Predestination

Eme Chijioke Eze

Predestination

Email: kize23@gmail.com

ISBN: 9785049655
ISBN-13: 978-978-50496-5-7

Published by Global Reach Publishing LLC

Printed in the United States of America

CONTENTS

DEDICATION

This book is dedicated to Sons of God who are seeking to discover themselves.

I thank Holy Spirit for His Help and I thank My Pastors who proofread this masterpiece, especially Pastor Thomas Sasser of Capital City Church, Mexico City and Shinnah. I am also grateful to Kalu Igwe Kalu who finally edited this great work.

Praise God, Amen.

INTRODUCTION

Genesis 1:1-4 *"In the beginning God created the heaven and the earth. And the earth was without form, and void; and darkness was upon the face of the deep. And the Spirit of God moved upon the face of the waters. And God said, Let there be light: and there was light. And God saw the light, that it was good: and God divided the light from the darkness."*

According to Genesis 1:1-4 as you study these verses, you will understand that there was emptiness, formlessness and darkness on the earth until the Spirit of God hovered over the waters and God declared light to be and light came. The movement of the Spirit of God preceded the declaration by God.

Hebrew 11:3 *"Through faith we understand that the worlds were framed by the word of God, so that things which are seen were not made of things which do appear."*

By declaration of His words, God formed the worlds. Confessing, saying or declaring words activates creation. I will call it the Spirit of creation. When you say any word, you create what you say. The Spirit of God, the carrier of the power of God activates every potential for example:

1. The Spirit hovered over the earth before creation.

2. He overshadowed Mary before Jesus' conception.

3. He descended on Jesus after His baptism to activate His ministry.

4. He came on the early church on Pentecost to empower them to be witnesses.

Acts 1:8 *"But ye shall receive power, after that the Holy Ghost is come upon you: and ye shall be witnesses unto me both in Jerusalem, and in all Judaea, and in Samaria, and unto the uttermost part of the earth."*

Acts 10:38 *"How God anointed Jesus of Nazareth with the Holy Ghost and with power: who went about doing good, and healing all that were oppressed of the devil; for God was with him."*

In Genesis 1:11-12 God created seed bearing plants and trees that bear fruit with seed in it and in Genesis 1:20-24 God made creatures that live in water, winged birds that fly and creatures that live on land. God put the seed of fruitfulness in all He created by blessing them.

Genesis 1:26-28 when God created Man, He blessed Man. God put in Man the seed of the blessings. Every word of God is a seed (*parable of sower*). The seed of the blessings of God in Man empowered Man to be fruitful, multiply, replenish the earth and have dominion. Man was engineered by God to succeed. The capacity to succeed is embedded in us. We carry seeds in us that we do not see. We have the seeds to replenish, subdue and have dominion. We are actually seeds. Everything God created is first a seed and then seed-bearing.

When Man fell by disobedience, they lost the power to do Genesis 1:28 anytime we sin, we lose the power to do Genesis 1:28.

We need to bring our lives under the Spirit of God, we need the Spirit of God to hover over our lives and then we make the declarations based on the words of God which carries the Spirit and Light of God.

We carry the breath of life i.e. the breath of God, so we have a portion of the power of God in us.

Genesis 2:7 *"And the LORD God formed man of the dust of the ground, and breathed into his nostrils the breath of life; and man became a living soul."*

We need to call it forth like God declared. We need to confess the Light of God on our lives, body, families, career etc. We need to frame our world with our words.

In our mouth lies the tree of life. In our mouth lies keys of the kingdom which Master Jesus gave us.

After creating and empowering Man, God engineered Man for Marriage. God desired marriage for and with Man.

Everything God created started with the Spirit of God hovering over and then Light, so for us to fully comprehend our purpose and destiny, we must understand the workings of the Spirit of God and Light. I want to state here that Light is a component of the Spirit of God.

Isaiah 60:1-2 *"Arise, shine; for thy light is come, and the glory of the LORD is risen upon thee. For, behold, the darkness shall cover the earth, and gross darkness the people: but the* L*ORD shall arise upon thee, and his glory shall be seen upon thee."*

The glory of God is in the Light. When Light appears, glory rises and darkness cannot comprehend.

Revelation 21:23 *"And the city had no need of the sun, neither of the moon, to shine in it: for the glory of God did lighten it, and the Lamb is the light thereof."*

When sin came, the Light and glory departed.

1 Samuel 4:22 *"And she said, "The glory has departed from Israel, for the ark of God has been captured."* (ES*V*)

The ark is the presence of God. The presence of God is in the Light of God.

CHAPTER ONE

THE PRESENCE OF GOD

In the presence of God, there is preservation, direction, voice of God, cloud of glory, provision, pillar of fire and rest. Moses only asked God for His presence. Joseph carried the presence of God. Jesus Christ is the presence of God, God with us now God in us. Emmanuel: God with us. The presence of God makes our life to be a Garden of Eden. The presence of God brings the rest of God. Since the absence of God pushed Man into the wilderness, the presence of God brings Man into the garden. When Man fell, they were cast out of the presence of God.

Aaron's rod budded, blossomed and bore almonds overnight because of God's presence. The presence of God brings life. Nothing dies in the presence of God. The ark was the symbol of His presence. The presence of God parted the Red Sea, pulled down the walls of Jericho and destroyed dragon.

In the Light they were blessed and empowered to be fruitful, multiply, replenish the earth and subdue it and have dominion over creation.

Genesis 1:28 *"And God blessed them, and God said unto them, Be fruitful, and multiply, and replenish the earth, and subdue it: and have dominion over the fish of the sea, and over the fowl of the air, and over every living thing that moveth upon the earth."*

In this book by the grace of God and the Spirit of wisdom and revelation, I hope to bring to light God's plans and purpose for every man.

For us to understand man and for any man to discover and deploy the potentials and the capacities already embedded in the man, we need to understand God's purpose for man. For example in a fish lies the capacity to be a fish, in a bird lies the capacity to be a bird, in a man lies the capacity to be a man.

CHAPTER TWO

DESTINY

LET`S DISCOVER OUR DESTINY

In God's Word lie His intent and His preordained intentions for Man.

We were created to obey God and walk in His ways. Deuteronomy 26:16-18 (*NIV*) *"The LORD your God commands you this day to follow these decrees and laws; carefully observe them with all your heart and with all your soul. You have declared this day that the LORD is your God and that you will walk in obedience to him, that you will keep his decrees, commands and laws – that you will listen to him. And the LORD has declared this day that you are his people, his treasured possession as he promised, and that you are to keep all his commands."*

Obedience is commanded and idolatry is forbidden. *Deut 4:1-39*

We were created to be holy. *Deut 26:19*

We were created to be blessed, be a blessing, be a nation and have a great name. *Genesis 12:3, Isaiah*

60:22

We were created to be stars. *Genesis 15:5, Genesis 37:9* Joseph was a star and his brothers were stars too.

Daniel 12:3 (*NIV*) *"Those who are wise will shine like the brightness of the heavens, and those who lead many to righteousness, like the stars for ever and ever."*

We were created kings and priests. *Genesis 17:6, 1 Peter 2:9* and *Exodus 19:6*

We are peculiar treasures. *Exodus 19:5*

We were created to dwell with God the everlasting Light. *Revelation 21:3*

We were created to be married to God. We are the bride of Christ. God is our husband.

Isaiah 54:5 *"For your Maker is your husband— the LORD Almighty is his name— the Holy One of Israel is your Redeemer; he is called the God of all the earth."*

Paul said in his epistles that we will be presented back to God as virgins and finally there is going to be a marriage feast in heaven with Master Jesus our bridegroom.

2 Corinthians 11.2 *"For I am jealous over you with godly jealousy: for I have espoused you to one husband, that I may present you as a chaste virgin to Christ."*

Revelations 21:2 *"And I John saw the holy city, new Jerusalem, coming down from God out of heaven, prepared as a bride adorned for her husband."*

We are the new Jerusalem- a city on a hill- a fortified city. *Jeremiah 1:18*

We were created to praise and worship God forever. *Isaiah 43:21, 1 Peter 2:9*

We were created to be the temple of God. *1 Corinthians 3:16, John 14:23, John 17:21-23*

We were created to be a house of prayer. *Mathew 21:13*

We were created to be a weapon. *Isaiah 49:2, Isaiah 41:15* and *Jeremiah 51:20-25*

Jesus Christ is our destiny because He is the Author and Finisher of our faith. We were created to enter into the rest in God.

We were created to be the light of the world. *Mathew 5:14*

We are made for signs and wonders. Jesus said signs and wonders shall follow us. Jesus came as a sign and we are signs. *John 3:8, Isaiah 8:18*

We are the image of God

We are the Body of Christ.

CHAPTER THREE

ADAM

God is our Maker, Manufacturer. He made us for a purpose. He foreknew and predestinated us. We were created for glory.

Psalm 139:14 *"We were fearfully and wonderfully made."*

Jeremiah 1:5 (*NIV*) *"Before I formed you in the womb I knew you, before you were born I set you apart; I appointed you as a prophet to the nations."*

Adam had unusual wisdom and power. God created man to operate from a place of rest. He operated from a place of rest. He named the animals, birds and fishes. He had unusual strength. All creatures were under his feet. He had riches, blessings, glory and honor of God at his disposal. He had the mind of God - a mind of possibilities.

We are like devices. There are many things inside of us we do not know how to use. We have a physical DNA and a spiritual DNA. Sin shuts out our mind to our spiritual makeup. When our minds are enlightened and renewed by the Word, we begin to understand our spiritual makeup. We have a physical destiny and a spiritual destiny. We were spirits before we became flesh. God is a Spirit, the Father of all spirits - creating us in His image means we are also spirits.

We are born again by the Word of God in Christ; we are also the word of God made flesh.

1 Peter 1:23-23 "*Being born again, not of corruptible seed, but of incorruptible, by the word of God, which liveth and abideth for ever.*"

Sin

Genesis 3:6 "*And when the woman saw that the tree was good for food, and that it was pleasant to the eyes, and a tree to be desired to make one wise, she took of the fruit thereof, and did eat, and gave also unto her husband with her; and he did eat.*"

They disobeyed in Genesis 3:6. The lust of the eyes, lust of the flesh and pride of life destroyed our first parents.

1 John 2:16 "*For all that is in the world, the lust of the*

flesh, and the lust of the eyes, and the pride of life, is not of the Father, but is of the world."

Studying the conversation between the serpent and Eve, you will understand that the serpent didn't have all the knowledge of what God discussed with Adam. He suggested, the devil cannot push anybody to sin and can only seduce you to commit the sin. Sin is seductive in nature. The choice lies with man. *"I call heaven and earth to record this day against you, that I have set before you life and death, blessing and cursing: therefore choose life, that both thou and thy seed may live:"* (*Deut 30:19*). We should avoid the voice of the stranger or self. *"My sheep hear my voice, and I know them, and they follow me:"* (*John 10:27*)

Prayer: Let the voice of the stranger be silenced with the Blood of Jesus Christ.

Points to Note About Sin

Sin makes us dust and makes the serpent to eat us at will. Sin made Adam and Eve dust. Serpents eat dust and serpents eat sinners.

Prayer: Oh God in the Name of Jesus Christ my Savior, I repent of every sin, I receive forgiveness by the Blood of Jesus Amen.

CHAPTER FOUR

THE COVENANT BEFORE THE FALL

God desires to be our Helper and you know Helpmeet is the first assignment of Marriage. God is our Helper and Husband. Holy Spirit is our Helper and Comforter. Who is a Helper?

A Helper is more able.

Just like He made woman from man, He made Adam from Himself and put His Spirit in Adam. His Spirit is a seed like sperm: a life giving seed. His Spirit in us is the seed in us that will help us fulfill destiny. Everything God created had seeds inside. His Spirit in us is the seed for dominion, fruitfulness and blessings.

God completes us. Without God, we are alone. We are complete in Christ.

Colossians 2:10 *"And ye are complete in him, which is the head of all principality and power:"*

We are the bride of Christ; we need to study

marriage from the Scriptures. There is a leaving and a cleaving in marriage for example, Abraham left his family, traditions and kindred to be able to walk with God. There must be total dependency and total surrender for a marriage with God to be successful.

No secrets or hidden things and no shame with God in all circumstances.

God is enough. He owns the whole earth. *Psalm 24:1, Hagai 2:28* and *Psalm 89:11*

God is our reward. *Genesis 15:1*

CHAPTER FIVE

MARRIAGE

THE FUNDAMENTAL TRUTHS ABOUT MARRIAGE

In Genesis 2:18 God said He will make a helper for Man, it's not good for Man to be alone.

In Genesis 2:24 Man will leave his parents and become united with his wife and they will become one flesh.

In Genesis 2:25 They were naked and felt no shame, the glory of God was there covering. The cloud of Glory was a covering for the Israelites.

The attack on Eden was against the first covenant (*marriage*)

In Genesis 3:1 The first cause of the fall is listening to other voices.

In Genesis 3:2 She disclosed a secret, an instruction.

In Genesis 3:4-6 Men wanted to be like God, wanted wisdom. They listened to God's enemy. They disobeyed and rebelled. Man lost the Spirit of God by disobedience thereby losing the blessings, authority and dominion.

Prayer : Father I confess every lust and pride, please give me the grace to be humble and destroy every lust of the flesh, lust of the eyes and pride of life by your blood in Jesus Name, Amen.

CHAPTER SIX

COVENANT

God's first intention for Man was the covenant or a covenant relationship or marriage and Gods last intention for Man is a covenant relationship. Adam and Eve committed idolatry or adultery.

Colossians 3:5 *"Mortify therefore your members which are upon the earth; fornication, uncleanness, inordinate affection, evil concupiscence, and covetousness, which is idolatry:"*

God sees sin as idolatry and adultery. When we sin, we have worshiped an idol. Sin comes from desires, thoughts and action. Through our thoughts we invite the demon in charge of the sin and he empowers us to commit the sin. When we sin, we have committed adultery.

Idolatry is adultery. When the Israelites worshiped and sacrificed to other gods or obeyed other gods, God said they have committed adultery. It is having anything to do with an idol, demon or gods. People may never carry idols but the demons now possess humans and make them disobey.

Prayer: Father in the Name of Jesus, I repent of every idolatry and adultery that I and my ancestors committed against you.

We are God`s temple

2 Corinthians 6:16 *"And what agreement hath the temple of God with idols? for ye are the temple of the living God; as God hath said, I will dwell in them, and walk in them; and I will be their God, and they shall be my people."*

When any demon possesses our body which is God's temple, they defile God's temple. Same thing the Israelites did. It's a kind of marriage. God calls it prostitution, adultery and idolatry. It is the second most important commandment and it provokes God to jealousy.

CHAPTER SEVEN

WALK OF FAITH

Let us understudy a few people who married God or had a covenant relationship with H*im.*

Enoch

He walked with God. Walking with God is the primary requirement for the covenant. *Amos 3:3*

What is walking with the Lord? Walking with God is actually walking in His ways.

Believing and obeying His commandments and laws is walking with the Lord.

Walking with God is faith and we can only please God by faith.

Walking with God pleases God. *Hebrews 11:5*

Prayer: Father in heaven, make me to walk with you.

Noah

Genesis 6:9 Noah walked with God.

Genesis 6:22 Noah did everything God commanded him.

Genesis 7:5 God remembered Noah.

Genesis 8:1 And God blessed Noah.

Genesis 9:1,7,9-17 And God married Noah i.e. entered into covenant with Noah and his descendants.

Abraham

There was a leaving, cleaving and total obedience.

Genesis 12:1-4 God married Abraham and his descendants as long as they remain obedient to Him. Abraham walked before God.

Genesis 15:18 The LORD made a covenant with Abram,

Genesis 17:1-14 Abraham was an intercessor.

Genesis 22:16-18 Abraham made love with God by obedience to the voice of God which increased his faith.

Moses

He obeyed everything.

Exodus 7:6, 10, 20.

Exodus 10:12-13, 21-22

Exodus 12:24, 28, 43,50

Exodus 14:26-27 He disobeyed once and it cost him entering Canaan.

The Strengths of Moses

Obedience, he carried the presence of God. He waited on God and encountered the glory of God that was why his face shone.

Exodus 33:12-21 God was pleased with him and he had favor with God. He was meek, the goodness and the glory of God passed through Him.

Exodus 7:1 He was a god to Pharaoh.

Exodus 4:21 God gave him power to do wonders.

Psalm 103:7, Exodus 33:13 God showed and taught Moses His ways.

He was God's right hand, A Symbol of authority.

Prayer: Father make me your right hand of authority. Make me your signet.

Studying the testimony of the Israelites' deliverance from Egypt, you will encounter many verses where it was written that God's mighty Hand delivered them and we never saw God's Hand physically. It implies that Moses became the right hand of God by obedience. You can become God's right Hand by obedience.

Exodus 3:19-20 *"And I am sure that the king of Egypt will not let you go, no, not by a mighty hand. And I will stretch out my hand, and smite Egypt with all my wonders which I will do in the midst thereof: and after that he will let you go."*

Samuel

Samuel grew up in the presence of God and always slept beside the Ark.

1 Samuel 2:21 Samuel grew before the LORD

1 Samuel 3:3 He grew in stature and in favor with the Lord and with men

1 Samuel 2:26, 1 Samuel 3:19 The Lord was with Samuel as he grew up and didn't let any of his

words to fall to the ground.

1 Samuel 3:21 The Lord continued to reveal Himself to Samuel.

David

He was a man after God's heart and he always inquired from God.

2 Samuel 5:19 God gave him rest.

2 Samuel 7:1,11 He lived a life of worship. He prays, praises and worships God lavishly. (*David's charge to Solomon*)

1 Kings 2:2-4 God testified of David that he walked in His ways and obeyed His statutes and commands.

The hearts of kings of Israel and Judah was not fully devoted to God except for a few like:

King Solomon loved the Lord *1 Kings 3:14.*

King Uzziah sought the Lord.

King Asa and Jehoshaphat inquired of God.

King Hezekiah.

Our God is a jealous God and His name is Jealous

Prayer: Jealous God, show me your Jealousy, show me that I am the apple of your eye. *Exodus 34:14*

2 Chronicles 16:9 *"For the eyes of the* L*ORD range throughout the earth to strengthen those whose hearts are fully committed to him…"*

Elijah had a right standing with God and he was a man of prayer.

Daniel purposed in his heart not to defile himself and he had an excellent spirit which came from the Spirit of God on Him.

CHAPTER EIGHT

NO OTHER GODS

You shall have no other gods before me and you shall not make yourself any idols in the form of anything in heaven above or on the earth or in the waters beneath.

God knew there were other gods (*demons*) who desired worship.

Exodus 20:3-4 and Exodus 20:23 He repeated it again. Israelites did not know the God who brought them out of Egypt. They forgot God's deliverance and murmured against God. They made and worshipped a calf. They prostituted themselves with demons.

God is holy and you can imagine how He took time to explain how to worship Him. He was trying to communicate to the flesh since the Holy Spirit has not fully come. He was looking for vessels that will be holy and obedient and He will speak to and through them. Obedience is a key to maintaining the covenant or marriage with God.

Deut 29:4 (*NIV*) *"But to this day the LORD has not*

given you a mind that understands or eyes that see or ears that hear."

Hebrews 12:15 (*NIV*) *"See to it that no one falls short of the grace of God and that no bitter root grows up to cause trouble and defile many."*

Deut 29:17-18 *"You saw among them their detestable images and idols of wood and stone, of silver and gold. Make sure there is no man or woman, clan or tribe among you today whose heart turns away from the LORD our God to go and worship the gods of those nations; make sure there is no root among you that produces such bitter poison."*

Deut 29:25-28 And the answer will be: "It is because this people abandoned the covenant of the LORD, the God of their ancestors, the covenant he made with them when he brought them out of
Egypt. 26 They went off and worshiped other gods and bowed down to them, gods they did not know, gods he had not given them. Therefore the LORD's anger burned against this land, so that he brought on it all the curses written in this book.
28 In furious anger and in great wrath the LORD uprooted them from their land and thrust them into another land, as it is now."

God married the Israelites; God remembered the covenant He had with Abraham, Isaac and Jacob. Israel disobeyed and forgot God and went after strange gods. God continuously warned the Israelites not to follow the gods of the land.

Prayer: Oh God give us the grace in the Name of Jesus Christ not to have other gods and forgive us in times past where we have followed other gods, Amen.

CHAPTER NINE

DO NOT FORGET

There is a tendency to forget God. There is a tendency to forget God's faithfulness and deliverances. God warned the Israelites.

Deuteronomy 6:12 *"Then beware lest thou forget the* LORD*, which brought thee forth out of the land of Egypt, from the house of bondage."*

Deuteronomy 8:19 *"And it shall be, if thou do at all forget the LORD thy God, and walk after other gods, and serve them, and worship them, I testify against you this day that ye shall surely perish."*

There is a tendency to forget the words of God if you don't meditate on it day and night. God instructed the Israelites to fix these words of God in their heart and mind, to tie them as symbols on your hands and bind them on your foreheads.

Deuteronomy 11:18-21 *"Therefore shall ye lay up these my words in your heart and in your soul, and bind them for a sign upon your hand, that they may be as frontlets between your eyes. And ye shall teach them your children, speaking of them when thou sittest in thine house, and when thou walkest by the way, when thou liest down, and when thou risest up. And thou shalt write them upon the door posts of thine house, and upon thy gates: That your days may be multiplied, and the days of your children, in the land which the* L*ORD* *sware unto your fathers to give them, as the days of heaven upon the earth."*

In the parable of the sower, you can be afflicted and persecuted because of the word. The devil can come take them from our heart. The cares and concerns of life can make the word to die. The deceitfulness of riches can choke the word.

Prayer: Oh God help us by the Holy Spirit to remember your faithfulness. Deliver us from every satanic agenda to steal your words from our heart. Uproot tares from our mind and deliver us from the cares and concerns of life and deceitfulness of riches in Jesus Name Amen. Give us a fresh heart and make our heart to receive your Word and be fruitful a 100 fold.

Traditions

Colossians 2:8 *"Beware lest any man spoil you through philosophy and vain deceit, after the tradition of men, after the rudiments of the world, and not after Christ."*

Every tradition is tied to a deity; the tradition of the Israelites is rooted on the word of God of which is the Ten Commandments. If the God we are serving is the God of Abraham, Isaac and Jacob, the God of the Bible and the Father of our Lord Jesus Christ, our sole tradition must be rooted on the word.

Abraham left his kindred and traditions. God was separating him from tradition. God is against tradition of the world. What is tradition and how did it come?

When Adam lost God at the fall, the devil introduced evil traditions, demonic worship and sacrifice on earth and darkness thrived. Man was created for worship and in their search for worship; they started worshipping sun, moon, stars, animals, trees, stones and even rivers. Every tradition on earth came directly and indirectly from the devil because Adam gave him authority to rule the world.

Mathew 15:3 *"But he answered and said unto them,*

Why do ye also transgress the commandment of God by your tradition?"

Why do you break the command of God for the sake of your tradition?

Traditions are rules taught by men. Mathew 15:9 *"But in vain they do worship me, teaching for doctrines the commandments of men."*

Jesus came to show us the tradition of the kingdom of heaven. Our Adamic nature is separated from our spiritual nature. All the parables of Jesus Christ started with the kingdom of heaven is like.....He came to introduce us to the traditions of heaven for example, the tradition of love and sacrifice. Even in the Lord's Prayer, we must request the kingdom to come in our lives, family and nations etc. and the will of God to be done on earth as it is in heaven.

Mathew 6:9-13 *"After this manner therefore pray ye: Our Father which art in heaven, Hallowed be thy name. Thy kingdom come, Thy will be done in earth, as it is in heaven. Give us this day our daily bread. And forgive us our debts, as we forgive our debtors.And lead us not into temptation, but deliver us from evil: For thine is the kingdom, and the power, and the glory, for ever. Amen."*

Tradition is slavery and bondage

Galatians 4:3 *"Even so we, when we were children, were in bondage under the elements of the world:"*

Prayer: Oh God in the Name of Jesus Christ, deliver us from the bondage of tradition, teach us the traditions of heaven Amen.

CHAPTER TEN

THE COVENANT OF GRACE AND LOVE

Jeremiah 31:31-34 *"Behold, the days come, saith the LORD, that I will make a new covenant with the house of Israel, and with the house of Judah: Not according to the covenant that I made with their fathers in the day that I took them by the hand to bring them out of the land of Egypt; which my covenant they brake, although I was an husband unto them, saith the LORD: But this shall be the covenant that I will make with the house of Israel; After those days, saith the LORD, I will put my law in their inward parts, and write it in their hearts; and will be their God, and they shall be my people. And they shall teach no more every man his neighbour, and every man his brother, saying, Know the LORD: for they shall all know me, from the least of them unto the greatest of them, saith the LORD: for I will forgive their iniquity, and I will remember their sin no more."*

The time is coming declares the Lord when I will make a new covenant with the house of Israel and Judah. It will not be like the covenant I made with their forefathers when I took them by the hand to lead them out of Egypt because they broke my covenant though I was a husband to them declares the Lord this is the covenant I will make with the house of Israel after that time declares the Lord.

I will put my law in their minds and write it in their hearts. I will be their God and they will be my people no longer will a man teach neighbor or a man his brother saying know the Lord because they will all know me from the least to the greatest declares the Lord, for I will forgive their wickedness and will remember their sins no more.

Ezekiel 36:25-27 *"Then will I sprinkle clean water upon you, and ye shall be clean: from all your filthiness, and from all your idols, will I cleanse you. A new heart also will I give you, and a new spirit will I put within you: and I will take away the stony heart out of your flesh, and I will give you an heart of flesh. And I will put my spirit within you, and cause you to walk in my statutes, and ye shall keep my judgments, and do them."*

God will cleanse you from all impurities. God will give us a new heart and new spirit and God will put His Spirit in us and move us to follow Him. The Lord will make you be like the Garden of Eden, loved and cared for by the Lord.

God said I am your husband

Jeremiah 3:14 *"Turn, O backsliding children, saith the LORD; for I am married unto you: and I will take you one of a city, and two of a family, and I will bring you to Zion:"*

And He will rejoice over us like a bridegroom rejoiceth over his bride

New Heavens and New Earth

Isaiah 65:17-25 *"For, behold, I create new heavens and a new earth: and the former shall not be remembered, nor come into mind. But be ye glad and rejoice for ever in that which I create: for, behold, I create Jerusalem a rejoicing, and her people a joy. And I will rejoice in Jerusalem, and joy in my people: and the voice of weeping shall be no more heard in her, nor the voice of crying. There shall be no more thence an infant of days, nor an old man that hath not filled his days: for the child shall die an hundred years old; but the sinner being an hundred years old shall be accursed. And they shall build houses, and inhabit them; and they shall plant vineyards, and eat the fruit of them. They shall not build, and another inhabit; they shall not plant, and another eat: for as the days of a tree are the days of my people, and mine elect shall long enjoy the work of their hands. They shall not labour in vain, nor bring forth for trouble; for they are the seed of the blessed of the* LORD, *and their offspring with them. And it shall come to pass, that before they call, I will answer; and while they are yet speaking, I will hear. The wolf and the lamb shall feed together, and the lion shall eat straw like the bullock: and dust shall be the serpent's meat. They shall not hurt nor destroy in all my holy mountain, saith the* LORD."

CHAPTER ELEVEN

JESUS CHRIST

Jesus Christ came with Isaiah 61.He fulfilled destiny. We have same Isaiah 61 anointing in us to fulfill destiny.

Isaiah 61:1-2 *"The Spirit of the Lord GOD is upon me; because the LORD hath anointed me to preach good tidings unto the meek; he hath sent me to bind up the brokenhearted, to proclaim liberty to the captives, and the opening of the prison to them that are bound; To proclaim the acceptable year of the LORD, and the day of vengeance of our God; to comfort all that mourn;"*

Take a quality study of Isaiah 61:1-2, it says <u>the Spirit of the Lord is on me</u> because He has anointed me to preach good news to the poor. He has sent me to proclaim freedom for the prisoners and recovery of sight for the blind, to release the oppressed to proclaim the year of the Lord's favor.

In Isaiah 11:2 we see some of the components of the Spirit that came upon Jesus.

The Spirit of the Lord will rest on Him-The Spirit

of wisdom and understanding. The Spirit of Counsel and Power. The Spirit of Knowledge and of the Fear of the Lord. These are the basic components of the Spirit that came upon Jesus Christ.

There are more components of the Spirit for example Spirit of love, glory, service, grace and supplication, obedience and faith etc.

Jesus Christ said as the Father sent Him so He sent us. He said we will do greater things than He did. Basically we need the Holy Spirit to fulfill our destiny.

The Holy Spirit is the custodian of the Light. He leads, teaches and shows. He hovered on the earth before God said. He came on Jesus Christ at baptism and Jesus declared His mission after the temptation. The Apostles received Him in Acts 1:8 before they can witness.

In Isaiah 61:2b-7, you can see we require vengeance (*spirit*) i.e. violent faith to access our inheritance in Christ Jesus.

Jesus Christ as our Pattern and Destiny.

Jesus is the Son of God and we are children of God.

Jesus is God and we are gods.

Jesus is the Way, Truth and Life. Our lives must guide others to the Way, Truth and Life in Christ.

He is the Resurrection.

He is the True vine and we are the branches expected to remain in Him and bear fruit.

He is the Light of men and we are the light of the world.

He is the wisdom and power of God.

His name is Power. *Philippians 2:9-11*

He is our Bridegroom.

He is with us.

He is the glory of God.

He is the Sword of the Spirit - The Word of God.

He is the Healer. He bore our sickness and infirmities and by His stripes we were healed. *1 Peter 2:2* and *Isaiah 53:3-5*

He is the Head of principalities and powers.

He is the Grace of God.

He is all the offering that is required for our Salvation: sin, guilt, fellowship, drink and whole burnt offering.

He is the Mercy of God.

He is Love.

He is the Holy Spirit.

Romans 8:9 *"But ye are not in the flesh, but in the Spirit, if so be that the Spirit of God dwell in you. Now if any man have not the Spirit of Christ, he is none of his."*

He is the Spirit of Creation.

He is the Spirit of salvation.

He is the Spirit of peace/rest.

He is the Spirit of remembrance.

He is the Spirit of comfort.

He is the Spirit of sacrifice.

He is the Spirit of servanthood.

He is forgiveness.

He is the only Star that shines in the day. The Bright and Morning Star, Daystar.

Luke 1:78 *"Through the tender mercy of our God; whereby the dayspring from on high hath visited us,"*

Jesus is compassionate.

Jesus was a Man of study.

Jesus fasted and prayed.

He had great knowledge. He is the wisdom of God.

2 Corinthians 1:24 *"Not for that we have dominion over your faith, but are helpers of your joy: for by faith ye stand."*

He talked with authority.

He had the Spirit of prayer, love, forgiveness and dedication.

He had the power to lay down His life.

He was merciful.

He lived a life of praises, thanksgiving and worshipping to God for example, He thanked

God at the tomb of Lazarus and before the bread multiplied.

He was rich. He had a treasurer.

Jesus Christ is our destiny.

He is our Shiloh (*Inheritance*)

He is our Sabbath (*Rest*).

Jesus Christ is the foundation of the Temple of God. *1 Corinthians 3:11*

He is the Grace of God. He is the fullness of God's grace

He is the Love of God

He is a Sign.

Return and Repent

Job 22:21-28 *"Acquaint now thyself with him, and be at peace: thereby good shall come unto thee. Receive, I pray thee, the law from his mouth, and lay up his words in thine heart. If thou return to the Almighty, thou shalt be built up, thou shalt put away iniquity far from thy tabernacles. Then shalt thou lay up gold as dust, and the gold of Ophir as the stones of the brooks.*

Yea, the Almighty shall be thy defence, and thou shalt have plenty of silver. For then shalt thou have thy delight in the Almighty, and shalt lift up thy face unto God. Thou shalt make thy prayer unto him, and he shall hear thee, and thou shalt pay thy vows. Thou shalt also decree a thing, and it shall be established unto thee: and the light shall shine upon thy ways."

Amen

Isaiah 55:1-3 *"Ho, every one that thirsteth, come ye to the waters, and he that hath no money; come ye, buy, and eat; yea, come, buy wine and milk without money and without price. Wherefore do ye spend money for that which is not bread? and your labour for that which satisfieth not? hearken diligently unto me, and eat ye that which is good, and let your soul delight itself in fatness. Incline your ear, and come unto me: hear, and your soul shall live; and I will make an everlasting covenant with you, even the sure mercies of David."*

Isaiah 55:6-7 *"Seek ye the LORD while he may be found, call ye upon him while he is near: Let the wicked forsake his way, and the unrighteous man his thoughts: and let him return unto the LORD, and he will have mercy upon him; and to our God, for he will abundantly pardon."*

Joel 2:12-14 *"Therefore also now, saith the LORD, turn ye even to me with all your heart, and with fasting, and with weeping, and with mourning: And rend your heart, and not your garments, and turn unto the LORD your God: for he is gracious and merciful, slow to anger, and of great kindness, and repenteth him of the evil. Who knoweth if he will return and repent, and leave a blessing behind him; even a meat offering and a drink offering unto the LORD your God?"*

Ye must be born again. *John 3:3*

You must return like the prodigal son to be able to access your inheritance.

Come unto me ye that are heavy laden, learn of me and you will find rest.

Galatians 2:20 *"I am crucified with Christ: nevertheless I live; yet not I, but Christ liveth in me: and the life which I now live in the flesh I live by the faith of the Son of God, who loved me, and gave himself for me."*

CHAPTER TWELVE

THE BLOOD OF JESUS CHRIST

Mathew 26:28 (*NIV*) *"This is my blood of the covenant, which is poured out for many for the forgiveness of sins."*

The first covenant was sealed with blood and the second covenant was sealed with the blood of Jesus Christ.

Moses was the priest of the old and Jesus is the High Priest of the new covenant.

Jesus ratified the new covenant with His blood.

He has redemption through the blood of Jesus (*Hebrews 9:12-28)*. Once and for all, by His own blood.

Jesus Christ paid our bride price with blood. *Revelations 5:9, Revelations 7:14*

There is no remission of sins without the blood. In the Blood of Jesus Christ activated the full power of God, the power of Holiness, the power of Resurrection.

It was the blood of Jesus that judged the gods of Egypt and freed Gods people.

Exodus 12:12 *"For I will pass through the land of Egypt this night, and will smite all the firstborn in the land of Egypt, both man and beast; and against all the gods of Egypt I will execute judgment: I am the* L*ORD."*

There is restoration, protection and judgment for the kingdom of darkness in the blood.

There is manna in the blood. Infact Jesus described Himself as the living bread, the manna.

The Old Testament is the shadow of the new.

He consecrated us, purged our mind and conscience so we can serve Him

Hebrews 9:14 *"How much more shall the blood of Christ, who through the eternal Spirit offered himself without spot to God, purge your conscience from dead works to serve the living God?"*

The blood releases the full power of God. The blood sanctifies us and makes us holy. The full power of God is activated in holiness.

It was the blood of Jesus shed at the cross that disarmed principalities and powers triumphing over them blotting out ordinances (*Colossians 2:14-15*). The blood activated the mighty power of God that resurrected Jesus Christ-The power of resurrection.

Ephesians 1:19-23 *"And what is the exceeding greatness of his power to us-ward who believe, according to the working of his mighty power, Which he wrought in Christ, when he raised him from the dead, and set him at his own right hand in the heavenly places, Far above all principality, and power, and might, and dominion, and every name that is named, not only in this world, but also in that which is to come: And hath put all things under his feet, and gave him to be the head over all things to the church, Which is his body, the fulness of him that filleth all in all."*

The power in the blood of Jesus swallowed up death in victory hallelujah.

The power in the blood of Jesus enthrones.

The blood of Jesus is the power that prevails.

Revelations 5:5 *"And one of the elders saith unto me, Weep not: behold, the Lion of the tribe of Judah, the*

Root of David, hath prevailed to open the book, and to loose the seven seals thereof."

When the blood of Jesus dropped, there was an earthquake, the saints were resurrected and the veil torn.

He gave us access. He tore the windows of heaven. The blood gave us access to appear before the throne of glory to receive mercy and grace.

Hebrews 4:16 *"Let us therefore come boldly unto the throne of grace, that we may obtain mercy, and find grace to help in time of need."*

Mathew 27:51-53 *"And, behold, the veil of the temple was rent in twain from the top to the bottom; and the earth did quake, and the rocks rent; And the graves were opened; and many bodies of the saints which slept arose, And came out of the graves after his resurrection, and went into the holy city, and appeared unto many."*

He removed the veil on the word of God and gave us access to the treasures behind the veil namely Aaron's rod, Manna and the tablets of the covenant.

He removed the veil and caused us to behold God's glory in His word and be transformed to glory by the Holy Spirit.

2 Corinthians 3:7-18 *"But if the ministration of death, written and engraven in stones, was glorious, so that the children of Israel could not stedfastly behold the face of Moses for the glory of his countenance; which glory was to be done away: How shall not the ministration of the spirit be rather glorious? For if the ministration of condemnation be glory, much more doth the ministration of righteousness exceed in glory. For even that which was made glorious had no glory in this respect, by reason of the glory that excelleth. For if that which is done away was glorious, much more that which remaineth is glorious. Seeing then that we have such hope, we use great plainness of speech: And not as Moses, which put a veil over his face, that the children of Israel could not stedfastly look to the end of that which is abolished: But their minds were blinded: for until this day remaineth the same vail untaken away in the reading of the old testament; which vail is done away in Christ. But even unto this day, when Moses is read, the vail is upon their heart. Nevertheless when it shall turn to the Lord, the vail shall be taken away. Now the Lord is that Spirit: and where the Spirit of the Lord is, there is liberty. But we all, with open face beholding as in a glass the glory of*

the Lord, are changed into the same image from glory to glory, even as by the Spirit of the Lord."

Jesus broke His body and became our access into the Holy of Holies. He is the High Priest and the sacrifice.

When the glorified Jesus Christ broke bread with two of His disciples on their way from Emmaus, their minds and eyes were opened to understand scripture.

Luke 24:31, 45 *"And their eyes were opened, and they knew him; and he vanished out of their sight. Then opened he their understanding, that they might understand the scriptures,"* The veil removed fulfilling one of His mission to remove the veil and make the blind to see.

Isaiah 25:7-8 *"And he will destroy in this mountain the face of the covering cast over all people, and the vail that is spread over all nations. He will swallow up death in victory; and the Lord GOD will wipe away tears from off all faces; and the rebuke of his people shall he take away from off all the earth: for the LORD hath spoken it."*

Isaiah 61:1-6 *"The Spirit of the Lord GOD is upon me; because the LORD hath anointed me to preach good tidings unto the meek; he hath sent me to bind up the brokenhearted, to proclaim liberty to the captives, and the opening of the prison to them that are bound; To proclaim the acceptable year of the LORD, and the day of vengeance of our God; to comfort all that mourn; To appoint unto them that mourn in Zion, to give unto them beauty for ashes, the oil of joy for mourning, the garment of praise for the spirit of heaviness; that they might be called trees of righteousness, the planting of the LORD, that he might be glorified. And they shall build the old wastes, they shall raise up the former desolations, and they shall repair the waste cities, the desolations of many generations. And strangers shall stand and feed your flocks, and the sons of the alien shall be your plowmen and your vinedressers. But ye shall be named the Priests of the LORD: men shall call you the Ministers of our God: ye shall eat the riches of the Gentiles, and in their glory shall ye boast yourselves."* We overcome by the blood.

Revelations 9:11 *"And they had a king over them, which is the angel of the bottomless pit, whose name in the Hebrew tongue is Abaddon, but in the Greek tongue hath his name Apollyon."* We reign by the blood.

Revelations 5:5-14 *"And one of the elders saith unto me, Weep not: behold, the Lion of the tribe of Judah, the Root of David, hath prevailed to open the book, and to loose the seven seals thereof. And I beheld, and, lo, in the midst of the throne and of the four beasts, and in the midst of the elders, stood a Lamb as it had been slain, having seven horns and seven eyes, which are the seven Spirits of God sent forth into all the earth. And he came and took the book out of the right hand of him that sat upon the throne. And when he had taken the book, the four beasts and four and twenty elders fell down before the Lamb, having every one of them harps, and golden vials full of odours, which are the prayers of saints. And they sung a new song, saying, Thou art worthy to take the book, and to open the seals thereof: for thou wast slain, and hast redeemed us to God by thy blood out of every kindred, and tongue, and people, and nation; And hast made us unto our God kings and priests: and we shall reign on the earth. And I beheld, and I heard the voice of many angels round about the throne and the beasts and the elders: and the number of them was ten thousand times ten thousand, and thousands of thousands; Saying with a loud voice, Worthy is the Lamb that was slain to receive power, and riches, and wisdom, and strength, and honour, and glory, and blessing. And every creature which is in heaven, and on the earth, and under the earth, and such as are in the sea, and all that are in them, heard I saying, Blessing, and honour, and glory, and power, be unto him that sitteth upon the throne, and unto the Lamb for ever and ever. And the four beasts said,*

Amen. And the four and twenty elders fell down and worshipped him that liveth for ever and ever."

The Blood of Jesus is the power over death. *Revelations 1:18*

The Blood of Jesus is the weapon we fight with to demolish arguments, pretensions and thoughts and strongholds that set itself up against the knowledge of God

The Blood of Jesus gives us the grace to remain in Jesus, the True Vine. *John 6:55-57.*

The Blood of Jesus Christ is eternal. He will make you live forever.

The Blood of Jesus is the Blood of God and the Blood of Jesus is God.

God said in Leviticus 17:11 *"For the life of a creature is in the blood, and I have given it to you to make atonement for yourselves on the altar; it is the blood that makes atonement for one's life."* And in Leviticus 17:14 *"For it is the life of all flesh; the blood of it is for the life thereof: therefore I said unto the children of Israel, Ye shall eat the blood of no manner of flesh: for the life of all flesh is the blood thereof:*

whosoever eateth it shall be cut off."

Plunder

The Blood of Jesus is the Spirit to plunder. The Israelites plundered Egypt when the Blood was poured on Egypt.

The Blood of Jesus plundered the Israelites from their taskmaster Egypt. It´s the greatest instrument for evangelism. It´s like a key, it binds the strongman of any kingdom and plunders the treasures of darkness. This is what it means by spoiling principalities and powers triumphing over them.

CHAPTER THIRTEEN

OBEDIENCE

What is obedience? It means believing the word of God, doing the word of God and walking in the ways of God and no idolatry.

It is in loving God with all that is in you, a perfect heart towards God.

Obedience is righteousness. Abraham obeyed and it was credited to him as righteousness.

Jesus teaching about adultery and murder made us to understand that the sin of adultery is committed when we lust and the sin of murder is committed when we are angry or bitter not when we do.

Obedience or righteousness and disobedience or sin begins from our thoughts.

It is wise we study the provisions God has made to help us in our obedience and understudy the strategies of the enemy to make us disobey.

We are what we think; we finally become what we always think.

Out of the abundance of the heart the mouth speaketh, evil deeds come from evil treasures in the heart.

How did the evil treasures get into the heart?

James explained how our desires brings sin and death.

James 1:15 *"Then, after desire has conceived, it gives birth to sin; and sin, when it is full-grown, gives birth to death."*

We will be judged from our desires and thoughts.

Obedience preserves. Obedience preserved Samuel and disobedience destroyed Saul.

Obedience is the key to maintaining our marriage with God.

Spirit of Obedience

God said in Ezekiel I will put my Spirit in you and you will do my commandments.

Since obedience is very vital in our walk with God

Jesus was perfect obedience. Jesus Christ is the Spirit of Obedience.

Philippians 2:5-11 *"In your relationships with one another, have the same mindset as Christ Jesus: Who, being in very nature God, did not consider equality with God something to be used to his own advantage; rather, he made himself nothing by taking the very nature of a servant, being made in human likeness. And being found in appearance as a man, he humbled himself by becoming obedient to death— even death on a cross! Therefore God exalted him to the highest place and gave him the name that is above every name, that at the name of Jesus every knee should bow, in heaven and on earth and under the earth, and every tongue acknowledge that Jesus Christ is Lord, to the glory of God the Father."*

Jesus said my food is to do the will of God i.e. obedience.

Without the word of God in your heart and in your mouth, you cannot obey God.

Joshua 1:8 *"Keep this Book of the Law always on your lips; meditate on it day and night, so that you may be careful to do everything written in it. Then you will be prosperous and successful."*

Obedience starts with believing and doing the

word. It is faith and belief.

It is rooted in hearing and understanding the word of God.

Obedience and Mind

It is from the heart. It starts from desires. Our thoughts are seeds. There are evil treasures/strongholds warring in our mind. We pull them down, we cast down imagination. Our mind is purged with the blood of Jesus. Evil treasures are uprooted

Mathew 15:13 *"But he answered and said, Every plant, which my heavenly Father hath not planted, shall be rooted up."*

Evil treasures hinder our communication and destroy God seeds (words) in us. We must renew our mind with the words of God. The word of God is a cleanser, when it's in your heart. It becomes a good treasure and it affects your thoughts and desires.

Proverbs 4:23 *"Keep thy heart with all diligence; for out of it* are *the issues of life."*

Philippians 4:7-8 (*NIV*) *"And the peace of God, which transcends all understanding, will guard your hearts and your minds in Christ Jesus. Finally, brothers and sisters, whatever is true, whatever is noble, whatever is right, whatever is pure, whatever is lovely, whatever is admirable—if anything is excellent or praiseworthy—think about such things."*

2 Corinthians 10:4-5 *"The weapons we fight with are not the weapons of the world. On the contrary, they have divine power to demolish strongholds.* [5] *We demolish arguments and every pretension that sets itself up against the knowledge of God, and we take captive every thought to make it obedient to Christ."*

Jesus' teaching about defilement said that It is out of the evil treasures in our heart that evil comes.

Evil treasures are strongholds.

Father let every evil treasure in my heart be destroyed by the Blood of Jesus Christ.

It comes from what we see, hear, environment, family, tradition, memories and experiences.

The eye and the ear are doors.

The heart is a door to the Spirit. It is the door to

the kingdom of God in us. Remember that Jesus told them that the kingdom of God is in them.

The heart is where God tabernacles *John 14:23*

According to Joshua 1:8, we must meditate on God's word day and night. It will empower us to do the word.

The word cleanses us. John 15 and the word in our heart prevents sin. *Psalm 119*

As the knowledge of God grows, as we meditate, grace and peace is multiplied. Remember it is the peace of God that guards our heart.

1 Peter 1:2 *"who have been chosen according to the foreknowledge of God the Father, through the sanctifying work of the Spirit, to be obedient to Jesus Christ and sprinkled with his blood: Grace and peace be yours in abundance."*

We have a task to consistently purge our conscience with the Blood of Jesus, Hebrew 9:14 *"How much more, then, will the blood of Christ, who through the eternal Spirit offered himself unblemished to God, cleanse our consciences from acts that lead to death, so that we may serve the living God!"* And uproot evil treasures/strongholds by divine power and bring them into captivity thoughts that are disobedient to the Spirit of Christ in us. Amen

2 Corinthians 10:4-5 *"(For the weapons of our warfare are not carnal, but mighty through God to the pulling down of strong holds;) Casting down imaginations, and every high thing that exalteth itself against the knowledge of God, and bringing into captivity every thought to the obedience of Christ;"*

Evil treasures/strongholds in our mind /desires block our access to the throne of grace. The devil uses evil treasures/strongholds like bitterness, unforgiveness, offence, anger, doubt, unbelief, envy, jealousy, hatred, murmuring and anxiety etc to block our access to the throne of grace where we can receive salvation.

Joy is a fruit of the Spirit. With joy we draw on the wells of salvation. With joy our service and offering are accepted before God. Without joy our harvest is destroyed.*"Therefore with joy shall ye draw water out of the wells of salvation."* (*Isaiah 12:3*) and *"The vine is dried up, and the fig tree languisheth; the pomegranate tree, the palm tree also, and the apple tree, even all the trees of the field, are withered: because joy is withered away from the sons of men."* (Joel 1:12)

In the first covenant the major cause of disobedience is the spirit of prostitution or whoredom.

Hosea 4:12 *"My people ask counsel at their stocks, and their staff declareth unto them: for the spirit of whoredoms hath caused them to err, and they have gone a whoring from under their God."*

And ignorance which cause them to murmur.

Voice of God

Hearing God's voice is an asset in communication or praying. We need the Spirit of wisdom and revelation in the knowledge of Him and the Spirit of faith to help us to believe, to open our eyes to see. The voice of God is always in the presence of God.

Only God's sheep hear God's voice. We need to recognize God's voice and differentiate God's Voice from the stranger voice or our own voice.

Father in heaven, make us hear your voice, make us be a sheep. Make us follow you in Jesus Name Amen.

Father, open our eyes and ear to see and hear you. Deliver us from every spiritual deafness and blindness.

I take authority over the god of this world who has blinded the heart of men. I command your eyes, ears and heart to be opened to the word of God.

Walking with God makes you hear God.

Obedience and love

Love is a spirit and obedience is the proof of love.

Our primary role in the covenant is to love God with all our heart, mind, soul and might and love our neighbor as ourselves.

John 14:21, 23 *"He that hath my commandments, and keepeth them, he it is that loveth me: and he that loveth me shall be loved of my Father, and I will love him, and will manifest myself to him. Jesus answered and said unto him, If a man love me, he will keep my words: and my Father will love him, and we will come unto him, and make our abode with him."*

John 15:9-10 *"As the Father hath loved me, so have I loved you: continue ye in my love. If ye keep my commandments, ye shall abide in my love; even as I have kept my Father's commandments, and abide in his love."*

Jesus loves us.

Obedience enables us remain in Jesus love.

John 15:11 *"These things have I spoken unto you, that my joy might remain in you, and that your joy might be full."*

It brings joy, complete joy.

Obedience is lovemaking.

Obedience is food. Doing the will of the Father is food. Every word of God is a command. It's not a suggestion.

Every Word of God is the Way. Every Word of God can slay because It's a Sword.

John 4:34-38 *"Jesus saith unto them, My meat is to do the will of him that sent me, and to finish his work.*

Say not ye, There are yet four months, and then cometh harvest? behold, I say unto you, Lift up your eyes, and look on the fields; for they are white already to harvest. And he that reapeth receiveth wages, and gathereth fruit unto life eternal: that both he that soweth and he that reapeth may rejoice together. And herein is that saying true, One soweth, and another reapeth. I sent you to reap that whereon ye bestowed no labour: other men laboured, and ye are entered into their labours."

Obedience and glory

Every time you disobey God, something in you dies.

The glory of God in you continues depleting as you continue to sin, you are dying spiritually until physical death sets in. You are falling short of the glory of God.

Romans 3:23 *"For all have sinned, and come short of the glory of God;"*

When you obey, glory adds and if you continue obeying, the glory multiplies until you become a Throne of glory and your face will shine (*light, transfigured, shining*) like Moses and Master Jesus' face.

Disobedience brings darkness and obedience brings light.

Obedience and Way

Jesus is the Way of God.

God teaches us His ways by empowering us to obey His word.

Enoch walked with God. God told Abraham to walk before Him and be blameless in the covenant. The Israelites were required to walk in His ways to continue to enjoy His blessings and favor. His ways are His commandments and statutes (*Deuteronomy 30:16*).

Walking in God's way pleases Him. Walking in God's way is obedience and faith.

You walk by faith following God in His word i.e. following His voice. Walking with God means following Jesus, knowing God, communing and communicating with God. Jesus said follow me. He said I am the way and nobody goes to the Father except through Jesus.

Moses walked in God's ways. God taught Him. It is essential that we ask God to teach us. *Exodus 33*

Isaiah 2:3 *"And many people shall go and say, Come ye, and let us go up to the mountain of the LORD, to the house of the God of Jacob; and he will teach us of his ways, and we will walk in his paths: for out of Zion shall go forth the law, and the word of the LORD from Jerusalem."*

Psalm 103 *"Bless the LORD, O my soul: and all that is within me, bless his holy name. Bless the LORD, O my soul, and forget not all his benefits: Who forgiveth all thine iniquities; who healeth all thy diseases; Who redeemeth thy life from destruction; who crowneth thee with lovingkindness and tender mercies; Who satisfieth thy mouth with good things; so that thy youth is renewed like the eagle's. The LORD executeth righteousness and judgment for all that are oppressed. He made known his ways unto Moses, his acts unto the children of Israel. The LORD is merciful and gracious, slow to anger, and plenteous in mercy. He will not always chide: neither will he keep his anger for ever. He hath not dealt with us after our sins; nor rewarded us according to our iniquities. For as the heaven is high above the earth, so great is his mercy toward them that fear him. As far as the east is from the west, so far hath he removed our transgressions from us. Like as a father pitieth his children, so the* L*ORD pitieth them that fear him. For he knoweth our frame; he remembereth that we are dust. As for man, his days are as grass: as a flower of the field, so he flourisheth. For the wind passeth over it, and it is gone; and the place thereof shall know it no more. But the mercy of the* L*ORD is from everlasting to everlasting upon them that fear him, and his righteousness unto children's children; To such as keep his covenant, and to those that remember his commandments to do them. The* L*ORD hath prepared his throne in the heavens; and his kingdom ruleth over all. Bless the* L*ORD, ye his angels, that excel in strength, that do his commandments, hearkening unto the voice of his word. Bless ye the* L*ORD, all ye his hosts; ye ministers of his, that do his pleasure. Bless the* L*ORD, all his works in all places of his dominion: bless the* L*ORD, O my soul."*

My Father in heaven, teach me your ways.

Blessings of Obedience

Righteousness is a seed and the fruit is glory and eternal life.

Deut 28 Obedience will make you increase in a land flowing with milk and honey.

Deut 6:3 *"Hear therefore, O Israel, and observe to do it; that it may be well with thee, and that ye may increase mightily, as the LORD God of thy fathers hath promised thee, in the land that floweth with milk and honey."*

Deut 6:5 *"And thou shalt love the LORD thy God with all thine heart, and with all thy soul, and with all thy might."* Love the Lord with all your heart

Obedience makes you sickness free and it will make the sickness go to your enemies

Deut 7:15 *"And the LORD will take away from thee all sickness, and will put none of the evil diseases of Egypt, which thou knowest, upon thee; but will lay them upon all them that hate thee."* Obedience makes you righteous.

Deut 6:25 *"And it shall be our righteousness, if we observe to do all these commandments before the LORD our God, as he hath commanded us."*

Obedience made Moses and Jesus an authority. It will make you a god.

Obedience and Death

Death to self is pre-requisite to obedience.

You become born again.

You die daily.

You are a new creation.

You deny yourself.

Unless you die to self, you won't bear fruit. Only when a seed dies, it bears fruit. The life of God in you is released when your flesh is dead.

The Adamic nature must be laid to rest for us to enter our rest.

We must become empty to experience God's fullness.

As we obey God's words, we are making love with God and He is inseminating us with His seeds and we will bear fruits of righteousness. When you obey God's Word, you bear fruits. God's commanding words are seeds. Jesus is the True Vine and we are the branches that bear fruits. We must be connected to the Vine. The Words of God must abide in us, remain in us.

How do we bear fruits?

We bear fruits by asking for anything and it's done.

CHAPTER FOURTEEN

WORD

Everything is a seed, *"While the earth remaineth, seedtime and harvest, and cold and heat, and summer and winter, and day and night shall not cease."* (*Genesis 8:22*) The words of God are the sperms of God. They are seeds. They reproduce the word of God. The word of God can become whatever He says. God makes us by making us His word and when we die totally to the flesh, we produce the words of God.

We are able to reproduce the Jesus in us in others the moment we die or are crucified with Christ and we become trees of righteousness bearing fruit of righteousness.

How do we make the word of God be fruitful?

Parable of Sower

In Mark 4:13, the Bible says *"And he said unto them, Know ye not this parable? and how then will ye know all parables?"*

Understanding the parable of the sower will

enable us to understand every other word of God and how it works in our heart to bear fruit.

Mark 4:15 *"And these are they by the way side, where the word is sown; but when they have heard, Satan cometh immediately, and taketh away the word that was sown in their hearts."* Satan comes immediately to take the word sown in their hearts.

Mark 4:17 *"And have no root in themselves, and so endure but for a time: afterward, when affliction or persecution ariseth for the word's sake, immediately they are offended."* Tribulation or persecution arises for the word sake and make them stumble

Mark 4:19 *"And the cares of this world, and the deceitfulness of riches, and the lusts of other things entering in, choke the word, and it becometh unfruitful."* Cares of this world, deceitfulness of riches and desires of other things enters to choke the word and it becomes unfruitful.

From the above scriptures, you will understand the intense battle going on against the word of God in your heart. I pray that the Blood of Jesus destroy anything fighting the word of God in our heart.

Mathew 13:23 But he who received seed on the good ground is he who hears and understands it, who indeed bears fruit and produces some a hundredfold, some sixty, some thirty.

Prayer: Father, we ask for an understanding heart to receive your Word causing it to bear fruit in Jesus Name amen.

Spirit of Wisdom and Revelation

We need the spirit of wisdom and revelation to see the word. He will teach you the word and lead you into the deep things of God and bring the words you have heard into remembrance. The spirit of wisdom and revelation helps you to be inseminated i.e. to get the honey out of the word.

Spirit of joy

We need the spirit of joy to receive the word and draw on the wells of salvation.

Spirit of faith

We need the spirit of faith to believe the word and confess. The spirit of faith makes the soul ready to receive the Word (*semen*). It makes the word fruitful, without faith the word will die. They believed because they had faith.

Salvation

You received and believed the word in your heart and you confessed with your mouth that Jesus Christ (*the Word*) is Lord and you were saved.

This is formula for making the word to be fruitful. When you receive, believe and confess the Word, salvation comes. You were born again by the word to become the word. It's a cycle. You were born by Light to become Light.

Everything God says is the insemination and what we do is the ovulation. Examples of do words are thirst, seek, walk, abide, worship, serve, thank, praise, come and hunger.

Faithfulness of the Word

God's word can't return void. *Isaiah 55:11*

God's word is settled in heaven. *Psalm 119:130*

Since day and night can't stop, God's word must come to pass. *Psalm 87:34*

Heaven and earth must pass away but God's word must remain. *Mathew 24:35*

God's word is more sure word of prophecy *2 Peter 1:19*

God's words are spirits. *John 6:63*

God's word is light. *Psalm 119:105*

God's word is wisdom. Psalm 119:98

God's word contains wonders of God. *Psalm 119:18*

God's word preserves. *Psalm 119:37*

God's word is a big spoil. *Psalm 119:162*

God's word can become flesh and money. *John 1:14*

God's word is a double edged sword. *Hebrews 4:12*

God's word is defense. *Job 22:25*

He is the Sword of the spirit. *Ephesians 6:17*

God's word is God. *John 1:1*

God's word is rock, fire, light and hammer

God's word cleanses *John 15:3*

God's word is health. *Proverbs 3:8, 4:22*

God's word delivers *Psalm 107:20*

God's word is fruitful. *Mark 4:20*

God's word is rest. *Hebrews 4:11-12*

Any action of God is the insemination.

Everything God created started with the word (*promise*) and ended with rest. He rested. The word is rest. Jesus the Word is rest. Jesus is the Lord of the Sabbath. Come unto me, all ye that labor and are heavy laden, and I will give you rest. Take my yoke upon you, and learn of me; for I am meek and lowly in heart: and ye shall find rest unto your souls.

When Man disobeyed God, they lost everything. Man became formless and empty, without direction. Man functioned in darkness.

Curses of Disobedience

Sin is a seed. The fruit is shame, sickness and death.

Disobedience is unbelief and sin. Obedience is

belief, faith and righteousness.

Disobedience will cost you the rest in God. The rest in God is the word of God. Jesus was perfect obedience. *Hebrews 5:7-9. Hebrews 4 = rest.*

Fear

It is a spirit and it's the nature of the fallen man. It makes you a prey.

2 Timothy 1:7 *"For God hath not given us the spirit of fear; but of power, and of love, and of a sound mind."* The Spirit of love, power and a renewed mind is the cure for fear. Fear thrives in disobedience. Live in obedience and the righteous are bold as a lion not afraid of anything.

God's presence suffocates fear. God always tell the Israelites not to be afraid that He is with them and He will not leave nor forsake them.

Perfect love casteth out fear. *1 John 4:18*

God commands us to fear Him. Fear God. He is jealous. Do not follow other gods or the gods of the people around you.

Prayer: In the Name of Jesus Christ, the Son of

God, I rebuke every fear in my heart. I receive the perfect love of God which casted out fear. Amen

CHAPTER FIFTEEN

HOLY SPIRIT

In Genesis 1, the Holy Spirit hovered before God said and Light came. Without the Holy Spirit we can do nothing, we cannot prevail.

1 Samuel 2:9 *"He will keep the feet of his saints, and the wicked shall be silent in darkness; for by strength shall no man prevail."* for by strength shall no man prevail. We cannot rise from dust; we cannot inherit the throne glory.

Zechariah 4:6 *"Then he answered and spake unto me, saying, This is the word of the LORD unto Zerubbabel, saying, Not by might, nor by power, but by my spirit, saith the LORD of hosts."* Not by might, nor by power but by my Spirit says the Lord. Jesus was anointed by the Holy Spirit many times. The apostles were filled with the Holy Spirit before they became witnesses and they were refilled many times.

He is our teacher.

He helps us in prayers.

He shows us.

He leads.

He sanctifies us.

He purges us.

He helps us in everything worship, service, obedience.

He is the custodian of the other spirits.

He helped Jesus to offer Himself for our redemption.

Holiness makes us a virgin and makes us ready for the final marriage.

Holy Spirit knows the mind of God.

He helps us remember.

He is the deposit that makes us know that we are God's children and know that we have inherited eternal life.

He is life and eternal life.

He makes us Holy

He is the seal of ownership.

He is the oil in the lamp of the wise virgins.

Glory

Glory is the fullness of God. It is the fullness of light. It is the fullness of Jesus.

There is glory in holiness. Exodus 15:11 *"Who is like unto thee, O LORD, among the gods? who is like thee, glorious in holiness, fearful in praises, doing wonders?"* Glory can only come on holiness. Holiness can come by the word of God. As you behold the word of God, you behold the glory of God and you are changed until you become the glory of God.

It starts with hearkening to the voice of God. It starts with believing and obeying the word of God. Mary and Martha believed at the tomb and they beheld the glory of God.

Romans 6: 4 *"Therefore we are buried with him by baptism into death: that like as Christ was raised up from the dead by the glory of the Father, even so we also should walk in newness of life."* Christ was raised from the dead by the glory of the Father.

Faith and glory

Jesus manifested His glory only where they

believed.

The glory of God breaks protocols. He provided the manna and parted the Red Sea.

The glory of God is the rest of God i.e. bringing heaven on earth. It is His dwelling place.

One of the works of the Holy Spirit is to sanctify us and make us a light.

The Glory of God directs-cloud of glory.

The Glory of God turns you into the glory of God.

Faith to glory *"But we all, with open face beholding as in a glass the glory of the Lord, are changed into the same image from glory to glory, even as by the Spirit of the Lord." (2 Corinthians 3:18*) As we continue to behold Him in prayers, worship and the word, we are transformed into His image from glory to glory.

He makes alive. He raised Lazarus. When Jesus heard that, He said, this sickness is not unto death, but for the glory of God, that the Son of God might be glorified thereby. *"Jesus saith unto her, Said I not unto thee, that, if thou wouldest believe, thou shouldest see the glory of God?"* (*John 11:40*)

The Spirit of glory

Jesus Christ is the Glory of God.

He is the King of glory.

The hope of glory.

Isaiah 60-the glory of God brings the wealth of God.

The glory realm is the worship and praises realm. 24hrs 60mins 60sec worship

The Glory of God opens a door no man can shut.

The glory of God will turn you into a nation.

Light and Glory

The Word of God is the primary source of Light. It's a lamp unto our feet. We are the light of the world. Jesus commissioned us light. We are children of light. When we dwell in light, we dwell in authority. Darkness will always shatter at the presence of light. Isaiah 60 Jesus is the glory and the light of God. He is our everlasting light. Every blessing is in the light. The light is the bringer of life. It destroys misery.

How to get the Light and the glory

When you receive Jesus Christ in you, everything the Light carries is in you because Jesus is the light of men.

The blessing is already in us and it is activated by Light; speaking and doing the Light. The light came before everything came.

When you continue speaking what God has said about you in His word or His audible voice or through revelation in light or in righteousness, It comes to pass and you enter into rest. The fulfillment of a particular promise is rest. Every promise is light and its fulfillment is rest.

God said let there be light and light came and He said other things and they came forth. Why did He start with light?

Everything was already there, It needed the light, illumination, knowledge to know what to speak or call forth or declare. Wealth, provision, dominion was there.

Prayer: Let the Light of your glory shine on me and shatter every darkness in Jesus Name Amen.

Let the power of Light in Christ Jesus destroy every darkness.

Let your glory arise on me.

Know Jesus, when you know Jesus, you know God. When you marry Jesus, you marry God. Your mouth is the key to victory. It's the tree of life. Declare and be justified, *"Put me in remembrance: let us plead together: declare thou, that thou mayest be justified."* (*Isaiah 43:26*).

When the Spirit of God comes on anything, you can say anything and it comes to pass.

Praise, Worship and Thanksgiving and the Glory

It brings God's presence and glory. As you praise God, God is enthroned and we are inseminated by His Word i.e. hear His voice because the tablets of the covenant were in the ark which signified His presence. His voice and the words are seeds.

When the voice of God departs, the glory departs.

Praise, worship and thanksgiving and joy keep the heart fertile and strong to receive the seed and bear fruit.

It's a heavenly seed. The Word or voice is watered by heavenly joy; Unspeakable joy of the Holy Ghost.

Praise incubates the word. As you praise God, you will dwell in His presence and He remains in you and you bear fruit.

The seed of God does not have a gestation period. The more the praise, the faster the reproduction. Just like Aaron's rod budded, sprouted, blossomed and bore fruit in God's presence. Any dry issue can be resurrected in God's presence.

Numbers 17:8 *"And it came to pass, that on the morrow Moses went into the tabernacle of witness; and, behold, the rod of Aaron for the house of Levi was budded, and brought forth buds, and bloomed blossoms, and yielded almonds."* God's presence is the incubator. The gestation period is now. Faith is now.

When you believe, you receive. *Mark 11:23-24, Mark 9:23.*

CHAPTER SIXTEEN

TEMPLE OF GOD

1 Corinthians 6:19 *"What? know ye not that your body is the temple of the Holy Ghost which is in you, which ye have of God, and ye are not your own?"*

When God says we are His temple what does He have in mind? God can't dwell in temple built with human hands.

When Jesus Christ was about to be glorified. He said in John 14:23 *"Jesus answered and said unto him, If a man love me, he will keep my words: and my Father will love him, and we will come unto him, and make our abode with him."*

When God comes and makes His abode in you, He comes with the Cherubim and all the host of heaven and they live in you. They bring their power, honor, glory, riches, strength and wisdom.

John 17:21-23 *"That they all may be one; as thou, Father, art in me, and I in thee, that they also may be one in us: that the world may believe that thou hast sent me. And the glory which thou gavest me I have given them; that they may be one, even as we are one: I in them, and thou in me, that they may be made perfect in one; and that the world may know that thou hast sent me, and hast loved them, as thou hast loved me."*

From the above scriptures, Jesus was speaking about the temple. When we obey God, we receive the love of God who comes and dwells in us thereby making us His dwelling place His temple. You will understand that you can't receive the glory that the Father gave Jesus until you become one with the Father and one with Jesus Christ by obedience. This is the marriage.

Jesus is the foundation and the chief cornerstone of the temple that God will inhabit. *1 Corinthians 3:11*

The Holy Spirit is the original landlord of our body. Any spirit residing in our body is a tenant and we have authority in Christ to quit them.

Jesus Christ: the Sweeper of the temple can sweep them away.

They can be uprooted.

And when enough light enters, they will disappear because darkness can't resist light.

They can be gathered as chaff by the Holy Ghost and burnt with an unquenchable fire.

Prayer: Father make me one with you and make my body your temple, sweep away every corruption and anything that defileth and burn them with your unquenchable fire.

Components of the Temple

There is precision in the temple. Everything was done in orderliness and according to specifications.

The Tabernacle in the wilderness, the Temple Solomon built and the Temple in the book of Revelations is same.

God has tabernacled in us. The cherubim and the entire angelic host are in us.

There is praise and worship in the temple.

We are houses of prayers.

There are blessings and riches in the temple.

There is wisdom

There is strength.

There is the healing river and tree of life in the temple.

There is everlasting life in the temple.

There is judgment in the temple.

There is mercy.

The Lion of Judah is in the temple and It's in you.

The Temple and the Glory

Exodus 33 contains some components of God's glory. When God knows you by name, you will find favor with Him.

When God teaches you His ways, you know Him more and continue to find favor with Him.

The dedication of the temple by Solomon preceded the glory of God. The dedication of our body which is God's temple precedes glory.

The presence and rest of God is in God's glory.

The goodness of God is the glory of God.

There are compassion and mercy at the throne of glory.

CHAPTER SEVENTEEN

GOD

We are the Image of God. He created us in His own image. In Genesis 1:26a, God said *"And God said, Let us make man in our image, after our likeness:"* For us to be able to understand ourselves, we need to understand the image of God that we carry. According to the scriptures, the cherubim are the closest creatures to the Almighty God and they are continually saying Holy Holy Holy worshiping God. They are very powerful angelic beings who guard and carry God around in case He wants to move. They have four faces. God is the Great I am, I am that I am. Because of the closeness of these creatures to God over eternity, there is a possibility that they have assimilated and adopted the features of God.

They bear the image of God.

They have eyes everywhere.

Discovering God and Recovering Our Identity

The first character of God that we saw in the

scriptures is say. As the **image of God**, we are expected to say: in this regard say means create. Before we can fully create or say things that are very good and enter rest like God did, we must allow the Holy Spirit to hover around us. We must be filled with Holy Spirit so that we can create Light.

Secondly, we are the **Body of Christ**, our eyes, hands, legs and voice are the voice of Jesus Christ. He said as the Father sent Him so He sent us. At His voice, Jesus performed many wonders: the lame walked, the blind saw and demons were destroyed and death was humiliated at the tomb of Lazarus, infact death died. The seas raged and roared but at the voice of Jesus Christ, they became calm. His voice makes seas to convulse. His voice is mightier than many waters. *Psalm 29*

He voice created money in the fish mouth. His voice made the fish come and Peter caught plenty.

He disarmed principalities and powers, how did He do it? By His voice in righteousness and the shedding of His Blood (*Colossians 2:13–14*).

In the Old Testament, the blessings on Abraham was transmitted to Isaac by voice and to Jacob by voice. Moses did wonders only by saying what God asked Him to say. David killed Goliath by what He said.

God told Jeremiah that He will make His Word be like fire and His enemies like word. *"Wherefore thus saith the LORD God of hosts, Because ye speak this word, behold, I will make my words in thy mouth fire, and this people wood, and it shall devour them."* (*Jeremiah 5:14*). By our words we are justified or condemned. Declare it so you may be justified. Jesus said He has given us a mouth and wisdom that our adversaries cannot resist or gainsay.

The spirit of boldness helps us in making bold declarations. The more you meditate on the Words of God and know God, you will get courage and you can make bold declarations like Joseph, Esther, Mordecai, Daniel Shedrach, Meshach and Abednego.

The declarations of Hezekiah extended His life. The spirit of prayer helps us to make these declarations. Our lives depend on it. The Holy Spirit is the Spirit of remembrance, He remembers these words stored in our spirit. He gives us joy so we can draw on the wells of salvation.

Prayer: Father we ask that you anoint our tongues with Fire, we ask for the spirit of intercession, the spirit that cries that Abba Father. Thank you Jesus.

With our hearts we believe and with our mouths we confess and receive salvation. Jesus Christ is the word of God. He is Sword of the Spirit. He is Spirit of salvation. Whenever we believe any word of God and confess that word, we receive the salvation that word brings. This is the foundation of our walk with God. This is the first thing we did when we received salvation. We believed that Jesus Christ died and arose for our sins and we confessed Jesus Christ as our Lord and personal savior and we received salvation. As we continue to believe the word of God and confess with our mouth, we will receive salvation.

When we receive salvation, we are saved from destruction.

Light in the beginning. God created Light and Jesus is the Light of men and life. He commissioned us as the light of the world. Jesus is the Light that shatters darkness. When we walk in the Light of God or in the ways of God, we destroy every darkness and its entire works.

Whenever the Word of God is spoken, it's like where the pool at Bethsaida is stirred. If you believe it immediately, you will receive the manifestation. If you are the first to dive in as the water is being stirred.

Create

We create with our tongues. Life and death is in our tongues. The major assignment of the enemy is to defile our tongues so the tongue loses power to create. There is power in your tongue. This is very vital, that is why the Fire that came is Acts 2 came as tongues of fire, it changed the speech of Peter and thousands were saved.

Prayer: Father cleanse my tongue from every filth. Send your Angel to touch my tongue with coals of fire to burn vain words and lie. Fill me with your Truth.

Prayer: Say I create the salvation of my family members, I create my healing, I create my peace and peace in my family. I create peace in my marriage, I create my new job. I create children and I create a successful business in Jesus Name Amen.

You can create anything you desire but I will recommend you create godly things and bring heaven into your families.

One facet of the face of God is an eagle face which each of the four living creatures named as Cherubim had. They are placed around the throne of God to protect its holiness and proclaim the glory of God when it is revealed to them (*Ezek 1:3-10; 10:15; Rev 4:6-10*). Each time the living creatures revealed a facet of God, we see the elders who represent the Church of God fall down before God and worship Him by casting their crowns (*Rev 4:9-11*).

In other words, whenever they realized their royal identity that God has lavished upon them, they humbled themselves before God and give Him all the glory for what He has given them because of His benevolence. Lack of revelation always deprecates the glory due to God, but abundant revelation glorifies God. The eagles represented the royalty of God. Because we are God's children adopted into His great lineage of royalty, we are called in the Bible as "*a royal priesthood*", "*kings*" and "*His own special people*" (*1 Peter 2:9*; *Rev 1:6*). As God's children we need to know deeply about this kingly lineage that we have and need to remind ourselves of it especially when we feel as worthless trash because of the devil's soulish ideas that come from the third rated world system of governance. Royals are always taught to behave and live in a royal way, which is totally different from the way people live outside of it. We also need to teach ourselves to think, live and behave like the royalty of God's family when we live in this world. We are in the world but not of the world, *"And now I am no more in the world, but these are in the world, and I come to thee. Holy Father, keep through thine own name those whom thou hast given me, that they may be one, as we are. They are not of the world, even as I am not of the world."*(*John 17:11,16*)

We are going to know about the eagle, because God has called us to be one with such royal characteristics to exhibit as long as we live on this earth. Because we are the ones who have a royal character of an eagle within us, we just need to learn what is inside us and remind ourselves of it when we feel otherwise. You might have heard about a story of an eagle egg which was placed in the crow's nest and got hatched by it. The eaglet did not know that it is an eagle and stayed with the crow in the lower altitude thinking of a crow by being with them. One day when it saw an eagle trying to attack the crow flocks, something within it said, soar higher and the eagle will get scared. Once the eaglet believed it can, it went after the attacking eagle higher and higher in to the high places, till it surrendered to the young energetic eagle. Surprised by the power within it, the young eagle left the crow flocks forever to live in the higher altitude of greatness and royalty. In the same way we as believers not knowing the royal lineage of our God have been living in the crow crowd of worldly people in the low altitude of the earth. But I believe as you come to understand the eagle face of the royalty of our

Heavenly Father, you too will soon believe you can and begin to soar high in your spirit into the heavenly mindedness of our God and live perpetually in the lifestyle of royalty. The crow-based earthly low altitude thinking of the old man is thrown away and replaced with the "*I can do all things through Christ"* (*Phil 4:13*) renewed high altitude heavenly thinking of the eagle for the glory of God (*Eph 4:22-24*). Remember the apostolic exhortation of Apostle Paul to soar in to high places by setting our minds on things above *"If ye then be risen with Christ, seek those things which are above, where Christ sitteth on the right hand of God. Set your affection on things above, not on things on the earth."* (*Colossians 3:1-2*).

1. Eagles Flock Together

As the old saying goes, "*Birds of like feathers flock together*". Eagles do not mix with other birds but always only enjoys flying in the high altitude of the eagle only. We as the children God are told not to forsake the assembling of saints but come together and encourage each other to live a royal lifestyle of God with other believers. This royal character of our heavenly Father and lifestyle is the heavenly attitude of high altitude sermon of Jesus on the mount (*Heb 10:25; 3:13; 1 Thess 5:11; Matt 5:1-48*). Also like Jesus, Moses and many other saints of the past, will go alone and pray with the Heavenly Father (*Matt 6:6; Exod 24:15, 18; Luke 6:12*). We soar alone in the spirit realm with God the Father many times.

2. **Eagles See Long Distance Prey or Enemy**

Eagles have strong vision and so are able to identify its prey and focuses on it until it gets the prey, and at the same time, it is able to see from afar its enemy the snakes trying to sneak in to its nest in order to steal its egg or to kill its young ones. Though eagles build its nest on high rocks and places, snakes have a tendency and ability to climb it. But the strong vision of eagles keeps the enemies away from its nest. We as the children of God are focused on our reward which is to kill the unbelief, sorrow, depression and eat the positive things of peace, joy and righteousness as a result of killing it (*Isa 61:2-3; Rom 14:17*). The demons and devil have a tendency and ability to attack our nest which is our home, finance, relationships, health, spiritual well being and soulish wholeness (*1 Peter 5:8*). The demonic realm of principalities, powers and rulers of the darkness of this age who are trying to steal, kill and destroy our abundant life of God within our families, loved ones and our community, we see by the foresight and strong vision of God from far off and start to resist it by attacking it, the enemy who tries to come in will become scared and flee away (*John 10:10*; *Eph 6:12*; *James 4:7*; *1 Peter 5:9-10*). The Lord will reveal the plans of the enemy within our spiritual foresight like for the prophet Elisha. When the Lord reveals the plans of the enemy in advance to us, the enemies of our soul will become frustrated, powerless and confused till they can no more attack us who are the people of God (*2 Kings 6:23*; *Matt 4:11*; *Luke 4:13*). This has recently happened to me in my life too. The Lord showed the enemy trying to kill a lukewarm believer whom I know very well in a vision. I prayed for him to be shown mercies and had peace after that. Afterwards I met his mother a few weeks later and she told that this particular believer met with an accident and if not for God's grace would have died on that spot itself. I told her the time that it might have occurred and she said that it was the same time he met with an accident. I praise God for the strong vision of royalty he gives to us in various times which outwits the enemies' plans completely.

3. **Eagles Do Not Eat Dead Things**

Eagles never consume dead things but vultures do. Because we are the ones with the royal characteristics of an eagle within us, Jesus said, *"For my flesh is meat indeed, and my blood is drink indeed. He that eateth my flesh, and drinketh my blood, dwelleth in me, and I in him. As the living Father hath sent me, and I live by the Father: so he that eateth me, even he shall live by me."* (*John 6:55-57*). His blood that we drink is our faith in the saving blood of Jesus and the flesh of Jesus that we eat is the words that He has spoken to us which we keep in our lives (*Matt 26:26-28; John 6:63; 10:27; 14:15*). We the believers are the one who eat fresh flesh of Jesus' words from heaven through the Holy Spirit's teachings which always makes us live His life on earth royally (*John 1:14; 6:63; 11:26; 1 Corinthians 2:13*).

4. **Eagles Love the Storm**

Eagles are the only bird that loves the storm. When all other birds try to flee from the storm and hide itself from the fierceness of it, eagles fly into it and will use the wind of the storm to rise higher in a fraction of seconds. It uses the pressure of the storm to glide higher without using its own energy. It is able to do this because God has created it uniquely with an ability to lock its wings in a fixed position, in the midst of the fierce storm winds. After a certain period of experiencing storms face to face, the eagles love to play in the storms. The storms in life that we as God's royal eagles face are trials, tribulations and temptations (*John 16:33*; *James 1:12*). As we face the stormy wind of afflictions in life, the Holy Spirit helps us lock our mind in a fixed position with the grace of God through faith in the finished work of the Cross, which helps us not to spend our energy but just stay in the storm and enjoy the lift and height of heavenly mindedness in a greater and greater altitude (*1 Cor 10:13*; *Eph 6:16*; *1 Peter 5:9-10*; *Phil 4:7*). After a period of time we start to love the trials because of the positive things of peace that we are able to experience in the storm and the heavenly after-effect of being lifted into great heights of spirituality and ecstacy in believing (*1 Peter 1:8*), which would not have been possible without it. This is the reason Apostle James said, *"My brethren, count it all joy when ye fall into divers temptations; Knowing this, that the trying of your faith worketh patience. But let patience have her perfect work, that ye may be perfect and entire, wanting nothing."* (*James 1:2-4*). We as a person of royalty need to take a quality decision of accepting trials willingly with joy because it lifts us into higher altitude of spirituality without us wasting even an ounce of energy. After we start to use all the maneuvers in the midst of storms, we will surely say, "*Bring it on with a stout chest and our head held high.*"

5. **Eagles Test Before Trusting**

The female eagle during courtship always takes a male one in to the air after picking up a twig from the ground and go to a certain height and will drop it for the male to chase it. Once the male catches hold of it and bring back, the female flies in to a higher altitude and drop it in the same way. This is repeated until the female gets an assurance that the male one has mastered the art of seriously picking up the twigs in real love and affection. Once they get hooked up in trust, the father and the mother eagle mate for life. And they work together as parents. Apostle Paul made it clear that we must enter the kingdom of God's parental and a lover's joy, peace and righteousness only through tribulations (*2 Tim 3:12; Acts 14:22; Rom 14:17*). God tests us through various trials in order to test our love for the Lord and purify it by making us learn obedience through suffering (*Ps 66:10; Heb 5:8*). God tested Abraham before he trusted Him as his dear friend for eternity (*Gen 22:1, 9-12, 16-17; Is 41:8; James 2:21-23*). Some of us try to test God like the grumbling Israelites did, which is totally a wrong attitude that arises out of our sinful soulish mind (*Exod 17:7*). God must be trusted because he is perfect (*Matt 5:48*), we need to be tested because we are imperfect beings who need to be purified through various trials, temptation and tribulations in order to be made perfect (*Rom 5:3-5; Deut 8:16; Mal 3:3*). Once the tests are over, God trusts us and establishes us for eternity ahead (*1 Peter 5:9-10*). This is a royal courtship with God that we must undergo in order to be established for eternity.

6. **Eagles Train Its Children to Maturity**

Eagles always build its nest on high places where the enemies cannot easily reach. God always sets his weak and lowly in mind children in high places far above the reach of the enemy by His sovereign power (*Matt 5:3-4; Job 5:11; Ps 91:14*). The male eagles pick up thorns and lay it on the cliff as an outer shell of protection and then it brings twigs to form another layer over it for ruggedness and agility. And again it places a layer of thorns over it for the nest to withstand enemies' penetration and then places a layer of soft-grass just before the inner most layer of rugs which completes the nest. The finishing touches for the nest is completed with its feathers kept over the outermost layers of rugs. In the life of Joseph, his circumstances and his place of stay was full of thorns. He was thrown into a well by his own brothers because of jealousy and was sold to some nomadic Arabians as a commodity, who again took him to Egypt and was resold as a slave to an officer of Pharaoh. From there he was thrown into a prison where his feet were hurt by the fetters and was laid in irons for no fault of his (*Ps 105:17-18*). The presence of God and His grace were the feathers that were always present all around Joseph who kept him inside the nest of thorns where he prospered and did not bleed to death by the thorns of his circumstances (*Gen 39:2, 21, 23*). When we go through the times of hardship and trials for no reason of our mistake, God covers us with His feathers and protects us under the shelter of His wings. And only there we find our refuge and His faithfulness becomes our shield and rampart in the midst of all our thorny and harsh circumstances (*Ps 91:1-4*).

Both male and female eagles participate in raising the eagle family. She lays the eggs and protects them; he builds the nest and hunts. All the members of the Trinity participate in the royal training of all believers. The Father loved us and sent His only begotten Son to transfer us into the kingdom of His Son Jesus Christ (*Col 1:13*), the Son of God died on behalf of us redemptively and qualified us to be participants of the training of the royals (*Col 1:14, 21*) and the Holy Spirit works as the agent executive and facilitator in ministering the training course of the royals (*John 14:26; 1 John 2:27*).

While in training, the mother eagle will throw the eaglets outside of its nest and the eaglets will get scared and will always try to come back into the comfort zone of the nest. Slowly the eagle will begin to remove the feather, rugs and soft grass inside its nest step by step so that the eaglets can be trained to fly like them. The eaglets may feel that their mother and father are doing cruel things to them as they feel the thorns prick them and make them bleed. Many times we as believers try to stay in the comfort zone of the old season that the Lord has kept us to grow for a time. But the Lord takes us into situations that may seem very cruel as we start to bleed because of the hardship of thorns we face in the new season, but the Lord's motive in doing it is to make our fears flee and teach us to soar in faith. Because of the thorns we feel inside the comfort zone of our old and outdated season, we slowly jump out in to the new season like the eaglets jump out of the thornynest.

Then the mother eagle pushes them off the cliff of their nest into the air. As they shriek in fear, father eagle flies out and picks them up on his back before they fall, and brings them back to the cliff. This goes on for sometime until they start flapping their wings. God said to the Israelites who faced consistent trials, tribulations and time of great testings in the transitory time of wilderness, "*You have seen what I did to the Egyptians. You know how I carried you on eagles' wings and brought you to myself.*" (*Exod 19:4 NLT*). God also said to them, *"For the LORD's portion is his people; Jacob is the lot of his inheritance. He found him in a desert land, and in the waste howling wilderness; he led him about, he instructed him, he kept him as the apple of his eye. As an eagle stirreth up her nest, fluttereth over her young, spreadeth abroad her wings, taketh them, beareth them on her wings: So the LORD alone did lead him, and there was no strange god with him. He made him ride on the high places of the earth, that he might eat the increase of the fields; and he made him to suck honey out of the rock, and oil out of the flinty rock;"* (*Deut 32:9-13*). God always throws us off from the familiar surroundings during the transitory time between the old and new season. This makes us to get caught in a great fall off guard and suddenly we feel as though we are going to die because of the great fall, but instead we are safely taken into His wings of our Heavenly Abba Daddy to find comfort from all our fear. Slowly we start to enjoy the fall and the fresh air knowing that we will be taken by the safe wings of God each time. As we fall like the eaglets into great trials and fall, the blood of Jesus starts to flow inside our wings and strengthens our faith in the protecting sovereign hand of the Lord over our life. The great things that happen during this time is that we learn to live in the so called danger of fall by our faith and also especially we start to enjoy the trials and tribulation (*Rom 5:3-5; James 1:2-4*). Fear of the fall flies away because of trusting in God's love and sovereign protection and we soar consistently flapping the wings of faith and learn to stay that way without toiling (*1 John 4:18-19; Gal 5:6; Heb 4:3*).

7. **Eagles Retires Until New Feathers Grow**

When the eagles get older and weak because of the worn out feathers which slows down its flight speed and maneuvers, the eagles retires away in the rocks and will pluck away all its old feathers until it is completely bare. It waits until a new set of feather grows and comes out of his body. It stays in the hiding place until all the new feathers comes back to make it fly dynamically and royally again without much effort or toil. Likewise, we take off our old man of soulish self after a season of flying in faith and wait in the presence of the Lord to make us rise up with the new feathers of faith from the new man by renewing our minds with the word of God (*Eph 4:22-24*).

This is what Apostle Paul spoke about when he said, *"But now ye also put off all these; anger, wrath, malice, blasphemy, filthy communication out of your mouth. Lie not one to another, seeing that ye have put off the old man with his deeds; And have put on the new man, which is renewed in knowledge after the image of him that created him:"* (*Col 3:8-10*). We need to wait upon the Lord in constant prayer of the secret hiding place of God's presence in order to be renewed with new feathers and be strengthened to mount up and soar again like young eagles in faith (*Is 40:31; Ps 32:7; 119:114;31:20;Matt 6:6*).

May we all live royally as an eagle and soar in our faith for the glory of God in our end time generation!

CHAPTER EIGHTEEN

THE MARRIAGE FEAST

Qualifications for the marriage. Jesus Christ our Husband, the Bridegroom took time to explain to us what is required.

Holiness: To be set apart and consecrated. Without holiness we cannot see God. Purity is required. We are expected to be virgins. Paul said he will present us back to Jesus as virgins and Jesus Christ is coming back for a wife who is without spot, wrinkle and blemish.

The Anointing: In the temple, God instructed to always burn word every morning and evening and fan it too. We must receive the word: the wood and fire: praying in the spirit daily. We must be filled with the Holy Ghost.

The parables of the ten virgins: we must have oil in our lamp.

We must be wearing our wedding garment which is a garment of purity and holiness and righteousness. We must be clothed with Jesus Christ all the time. He is our righteousness.

Faithfulness: Service in the parable of the talents. God judged his servants based on their faithfulness to His instructions.

Charity, love, in the parable of the sheep and goat. God judged His servants based on the their giving to the needy, the sick, the prisoners, the naked, the thirsty and the hungry.

Wise and faithful servant: We need to do the words of God we have heard thereby building our lives on the Rock of Ages which cannot be shaken by the storms of life. This is wisdom *Mathew 7:24–27*.

Who then is the faithful and wise servant, whom the master has put in charge of the servants in his household to give them their food at the proper time? Mathew 24: 45

Jesus Christ asked Peter to feed His flock Read *John 21:15– 17*.

Faithful servants feed God's sheep.

Prayer and Faith: Jesus Christ in Luke 18:1-8 said we ought always to pray and not faint and in verse 8, He asked whether the Son of Man will find faith on earth when He returns. Prayer is communication and confession. We need the spirit of grace and supplication to pray effectively. The Holy Spirit helps us in intercession. *Romans 8:26, Ephesians 6:18* we need to build our faith by praying in the Holy Ghost. *Jude 20*

Benefits of Prayer:

The altar of prayer is where we obtain mercy and grace.

The altar of prayer is the altar of empowerment.

The altar of prayer is the altar of breakthrough and restoration.

The altar of prayer is the altar of glory. We are transformed and transfigured.

The prayer grace sustains other graces and makes them to be efficient.

Time of the Feast

Jesus warned that He will come like a thief in the night. The time may be in the night.

The Holy Spirit knows the time. He knows the

mind of God.

The entire ordained feasts in ancient Israel was meant to be a lasting ordinance. It was a prophecy.

God's primary focus is the salvation of people and their worship of Him. The Bible tells us that God created man to live with Him, and that God's desire is to reveal the riches of His grace to man throughout all eternity.

Ephesians 2:7 *"That in the ages to come he might shew the exceeding riches of his grace in his kindness toward us through Christ Jesus."*

To get this point across to the people of Israel, God set aside several religious holidays. Note some important points about the annual feasts or festivals:

- These holidays focused upon the salvation and redemption of man and the worship of God
- The holidays painted the prophetic picture of salvation, the salvation that God was to bring to man through His Son, the Lord Jesus Christ.

- God used the annual festivals to show a believer how he was to walk day by day throughout life.

I. Introduction to the Feasts of the LORD *Leveticus 23:1-2*

A. Sacred Assemblies-Holidays-Festivals of the LORD:

1. The festivals were appointed or set by God; they were sacred or holy assemblies that were held on very special holidays.

2. The festivals were a time when the people came together for worship and the celebration of significant events.

3. They were religious holidays that celebrated holy events. Consequently, the holidays included a time for worship as well as a time for great joy and festivity.

4. Only one festival involved mourning; that was the Day of Atonement.

B. Man may set aside a day for celebration, but only God can make a day holy.

1. Note the term "*my feast*" or "*my appointed feast*."

2. These were feasts that were appointed or set by God.

3. They were God's feasts, the appointed and set feasts of the LORD.

4. Again, only God can make a time truly holy, for God is the sovereign LORD of time.

5. God alone can take a period of time and make it holy, a time set aside for true worship and joyful celebration in the Spirit of God.

6. This is what God did with the annual feast or festivals of worship.

7. He appointed a time for special worship and joyful celebration of significant events (*Acts 17:24-27*).

Acts 17:24-27 "*God that made the world and all things therein, seeing that he is Lord of heaven and earth, dwelleth not in temples made with hands; Neither is worshipped with men's hands, as though he needed any thing, seeing he giveth to all life, and breath, and all things; And hath made of one blood all nations of men for to dwell on all the face of the earth, and hath determined the times before appointed, and the bounds of their habitation; That they should seek the Lord, if haply they might feel after him, and find him, though he be not far from every one of us:*"

II. The Sabbath v3

A. There was the Sabbath day of rest, the very first day appointed and set aside by God.

1. The Sabbath day of rest is actually the most important day set aside by God.

2. It is pre-Mosaic, stretching all the way back to the beginning of creation.

3. Right after creating the universe, God blessed the Sabbath day and set it apart for rest and worship (*Gen.2:3*).

B. Note this Scripture: God tells man to work six days, then he is to rest on the seventh day.

1. The seventh day is the Lord's Day, a day that God has set aside to be His day, a day in which man is to focus entirely upon the LORD.

2. The Sabbath day is to be a day of rest.

a. The Sabbath day is for complete rest.

b. It is to be a day of physical restoration, a day when the human body is allowed to restore itself.

c. Man's mind and body need to relax and rest;

to be free from the duties, responsibilities, pressure and tensions of day to day work.

d. For this purpose, God set aside the Sabbath day for complete rest and relaxation.

3. The Sabbath rest is a symbol of the spiritual rest that God promises to those who believe and follow Him.

a. The Sabbath rest is a symbol of redemption, of God's deliverance from the heavy burdens and trials of this life.

Heb 4:9-11 "*There remaineth therefore a rest to the people of God. For he that is entered into his rest, he also hath ceased from his own works, as God did from his. Let us labour therefore to enter into that rest, lest any man fall after the same example of unbelief.*"

Mat 11:28 "*Come unto me, all ye that labour and are heavy laden, and I will give you rest.*"

Exo 20:8 "*Remember the sabbath day, to keep it holy.*"

Exo 20:11 "*For in six days the LORD made heaven and earth, the sea, and all that in them is, and rested the seventh day: wherefore the LORD blessed the sabbath day, and hallowed it.*"

4. The Sabbath day is a day set aside for worship.

a. Note exactly what this verse says: the Sabbath day is a day of holy convocation, a day of sacred assembly, a day when God's people are to come together and assemble for worship.

b. In Deuteronomy 5:15, God told His people what the focus of their worship was to be: they were to focus upon their redemption from Egypt.

c. Remember: for the Christian believer, Egypt is a symbol of the world.

d. Therefore, the focus of worship is to be upon God's redemption, His salvation and deliverance from the world and its enslavements.

"Who delivered us from so great a death, and doth deliver: in whom we trust that he will yet deliver us" (2 *Cor.1:10*).

"Forasmuch then as the children are partakers of flesh and blood, he also himself likewise took part of the same; that through death he might destroy him that had the power of death, that is, the devil; And

deliver them who through fear of death were all their lifetime subject to bondage." (*Heb.2:14-15*).

III. The Three Spring Feasts: Passover; Feast of Unleavened Bread, and Feast of First fruits.

These three feasts were closely connected, taking place during an eight day holiday period.

- The Passover took place on the first day (the fourteenth day of the first month).
- Then on the very next day the Festival of Unleavened Bread began and lasted for seven days.
- The Festival of First fruits was celebrated on the day after the Sabbath, which is Sunday.

A. The Festival of the Passover (*v.5*)

1. The Passover celebrated God's great deliverance of His people from Egyptian slavery.

a. God had told His people that He was going to execute severe judgment upon the Egyptians.

b. He was going to send the angel of death throughout the land and execute the firstborn son of every Egyptian family.

c. Then and only then would Pharaoh release God's people from their four hundred years of enslavement.

d. But God's people could escape the judgments.

e. How? By believing God and trusting the blood of the sacrificial substitute.

f. God did just that: Note: Ex. 12:23-27

2. The Passover is a symbol of Jesus Christ, our Passover who was sacrificed for us.

3. Jesus Christ is the perfect fulfillment of the Passover Lamb that was slain on behalf of God's people.

4. Through the blood of Jesus Christ, a person escapes the judgment of God. God accepts the blood of the substitute sacrifice as full payment for the sins committed by a person.

5. Note that the Passover is His sign or prophetic picture of the coming Savior, of His salvation and redemption.

"The next day John seeth Jesus coming unto

him, and saith, Behold the Lamb of God, which taketh away the sin of the world." (Jn.1:29)

"Purge out therefore the old leaven, that ye may be a new lump, as ye are unleavened. For even Christ our Passover is sacrificed for us." (1 *Cor.5:7)*

"Who gave himself for our sins, that he might deliver us from this present evil world, according to the will of God and our Father." (*Gal.1:4*)

"And walk in love, as Christ also hath loved us, and hath given himself for us an offering and a sacrifice to God for a sweet-smelling savour." (Eph.5:2)

"Who gave himself for us, that he might redeem us from all iniquity, and purify unto himself a peculiar people, zealous of good works." (*Tit.2:14*)

"Forasmuch as ye know that ye were not redeemed with corruptible things, as silver and gold, from your vain conversation received by tradition from your fathers; But with the precious blood of Christ, as of a lamb without blemish and without spot." (1 *Pt.1:18-19*)

"But he was wounded for our transgressions; he was bruised for our iniquities: the chastisement of our peace was upon him; and with his stripes we are healed. All we like sheep have gone astray; we have turned everyone to his own way; and the LORD hath laid on him the iniquity of us all. He was oppressed, and he was afflicted, yet he opened not his mouth: he is brought as a lamb to the slaughter, and as a sheep before her shearers is dumb, so he openeth not his mouth." (*Is.53:5-7*).

B. There was the Festival of Unleavened Bread (*v.6-8*)

1. This festival recalled the need and urgency of God's people to leave Egypt.

a. After God's hand of judgment fell, events moved rapidly.

b. The Egyptians were desperate for Pharaoh to release the Israelites and get rid of them.

c. In fact, the Israelites were forced to leave so quickly that they had no time to adequately prepare.

d. They did not even have time to let their

dough rise; they had no time to put yeast or leaven in their bread.

e. They were forced to take unleavened bread.

f. There was the need and the urgency to get out of Egypt immediately.

g. This is a symbol of a believer's need and urgency to be freed from the world.

2. Note the facts given in this passage concerning the Feast or Festival of Unleavened Bread.

a. The festival was to begin on the day after Passover.

b. For seven days the people were to eat unleavened bread, bread made without any yeast whatsoever (v.6).

c. They were to assemble or gather together on the first day of worship.

d. They were to do no regular work on that day (v. 7).

e. The people were to approach God for atonement on each of the seven days, for reconciliation and forgiveness of sins (v.8).

f. Scripture tells us elsewhere that the offerings were to be a Burnt Offering and a Sin Offering.

g. Note: Numbers 28:16-25,

The people were to assemble on the seventh day for worship.

3. The Feast or Festival of Unleavened Bread paints a clear picture for the believer.
a. It symbolizes the need and urgency for the believer to be freed from the world and its enslavement to sin and death.

b. There is a need? An urgent desperate need? To be delivered from all the oppressions and pollutions of this world, from all the sin and evil, immorality and lawlessness, corruption and death of this world.

c. There is a need and urgency to be set free and liberated to live for God.

d. There is a desperate need and urgency to begin the march to the promised land of heaven.

e. Note the prophetic picture:

1) The Passover pictures salvation, deliverance, and redemption.

2) The Festival of Unleavened Bread pictures the immediate need and urgency to begin the march to the Promised Land.

3) Several Scriptures speak of the urgency for deliverance.

"Seek ye the LORD while he may be found, call ye upon him while he is near." (1s.55:6)

"... Behold, now is the accepted time; behold, now is the day of salvation." (2 Cor. 6:2)

"But this I say, brethren, the time is short." (1 Cor.7:29)

"See then that ye walk circumspectly, not as fools, but as wise, redeeming the time, because the days are evil." (Eph.5:15-16)

"For our conversation [citizenship] is in heaven; from whence also we look for the Saviour, the Lord Jesus Christ." (Ph.3:20)

"Henceforth there is laid up for me a crown of righteousness, which the LORD, the righteous judge, shall give me at that day: and not to me only, but unto them also that love his

appearing." (*2 Tim. 4:8*)

C. There was the Festival of First fruits (*v.9-14*)

1. This festival was to thank God for the crops, for the harvest of food that gave people life.

2. This was a symbol of Christ's resurrection: He is the first of the harvest, the first to arise from the dead.

3. Note some specifics concerning this feast.

a. This festival could not begin until the people had entered the Promised Land (*v. 10*)

b. They, of course, could not plant crops out in the desert while they were marching to the Promised Land.

c. Once they arrived and began planting crops, they were to give the first of their harvest to the LORD during this festival.

d. They were to take a sheaf, that is, a stalk, here and there, bundle it together, and bring it to the priest.

e. He was then to take the sheaf and wave it

as an offering before the LORD.

f. This was to be done on the day after the Sabbath, which would be Sunday.

g. After giving the wave offering to the LORD, the priest was to approach God for atonement through a special Burnt Offering.

h. Note also that a special Grain Offering was to be offered to the LORD, a Grain Offering two times larger than usual.

4. The result:

a. The aroma of the burning sacrifice and Grain Offering ascended up, symbolizing God's acceptance.

b. He was pleased with the aroma of the sacrifice, the obedience of the people.

c. But, there was one clear prohibition: the people had to put God first.

d. They were not to eat any of the harvest until the First fruit Offering was given to God.

e. This was to be a permanent law for all the generations to come, no matter where the

Israelites lived.

5. The application for us today.

a. The believer is to give God the first of his harvest, the first of his income.

b. He is to tithe, for the tithe belongs to the LORD.

c. The tithe should be an expression of appreciation and thanksgiving to God, for God is the One who has given us all that we have.

d. Our crops and jobs are due to Him; so is our health that enables us to work and earn a living.

e. We are to honor God by giving Him the first fruits to support the local church and the work of God around the world.

"Upon the first day of the week let every one of you lay by him in store, as God hath prospered him, that there be no gatherings when I come." (1 Cor.16:2)

"But this I say, He which soweth sparingly shall reap also sparingly; and he which soweth bountifully shall reap also bountifully. Every

man according as he purposeth in his heart, so let him give; not grudgingly, or of necessity: for God loveth a cheerful giver." (2 Cor.*9:6, 7*).

"And all the tithe of the land, whether of the seed of the land, or of the fruit of the tree, is the LORD's: it is holy unto the LORD." (*Lev.27:30*)

"Every man shall give as he is able, according to the blessing of the LORD thy God which he hath given thee." (*Dt.16:17*)

"Bring ye all the tithes into the storehouse, that there may be meat in mine house, and prove me now herewith, saith the LORD of hosts, if I will not open you the windows of heaven, and pour you out a blessing, that there shall not be room enough to receive it." (*Mal.3:10*)

6. The Festival of First fruits is also a symbol of the LORD's resurrection.

a. Christ is the first of the harvest, the first to arise from the dead.

b. It is Jesus Christ and His resurrection that gives the believer hope of arising from the dead to live eternally with God.

c. The prophetic picture of salvation is this:

1) The Passover symbolized the believer's deliverance or redemption from the world.

2) The Festival of Unleavened Bread symbolized the urgency of the believer to leave the world to begin his march to the Promised Land.

3) The Festival of First fruits symbolizes the glorious hope the believer has as he marches toward the promise land, the hope of being raised from the dead to live eternally with God, All because of the resurrection of Christ.

"That Christ should suffer, and that he should be the first that should rise from the dead, and should show light unto the people and to the Gentiles." (*Acts 26:23*)

"But now is Christ risen from the dead, and become the first fruits of them that slept. For since by man came death, by man came also the resurrection of the dead. For as in Adam all die, even so in Christ shall all be made alive. But every man in his own order: Christ the first fruits; afterward they that are Christ's at his coming." (*1 Cor.15:20-23*)

"Knowing that he which raised up the Lord Jesus shall raise up us also by Jesus, and shall present us with you." (2 Cor.4:14)

"Blessed be the God and Father of our Lord Jesus Christ, which according to his abundant mercy hath begotten us again unto a lively hope by the resurrection of Jesus Christ from the dead, To an inheritance incorruptible, and undefiled, and that fadeth not away, reserved in heaven for you." (1 Pt.1:3-4)

IV. The Feast of Pentecost or Harvest (*v15-22*)

- The purpose of this festival was to give thanksgiving to God for the harvest and to dedicate one's life anew to God.
- The Festival of Harvest (*Ex.23:16*) is sometimes called "The Feast of Weeks" or *"The First fruits of the Wheat Harvest."* (*Ex.34:22*)
- The festival is also a prophetic symbol of the great harvest of souls that took place when the Holy Spirit came upon the disciples in the upper room (*Acts 2:1*)

- It was a joyful occasion celebrating the end of the harvest season and dedicating one's life anew to God.

A. Historic observation.

1. The people were to give a wave offering of First fruits to the LORD, using two fresh loaves of bread (*v. 17*)

2. In this particular offering, leavened bread (bread with yeast) had to be brought (*Lev. 2: 11; cp. 7:13*)

3. The people were to approach God for atonement, seeking God's reconciliation and acceptance through the Burnt Offering (*v. 18*)

a. Note that they were to sacrifice seven male lambs, one young bull and two rams - all with no defect.

b. Remember that the number seven symbolizes completion, fulfillment, and perfection.

c. This was a symbol of Christ, His perfect and sinless sacrifice.

4. The people had to approach God through

the sacrifice of the Sin Offering and another sacrifice for the Fellowship and Peace Offering (*v. 19*)

5. The people were to have the priest take the animal sacrifices and wave them before the LORD as a wave offering, together with the bread of the First fruits.

6. Note that these were holy offerings belonging to the priest (*v.20*)

7. The people were to declare a sacred assembly on that day: they were to take a day of rest and gather together for worship (*v.21*)

8. The people were to make this a permanent, lasting law for all generations (*v.21*)

9. The people were to help and to protect the poor.

10. How? When they reaped the harvest, they were to leave enough for the poor to enter the fields to gather food for survival (*v.22*)

B. The Prophetic Application.

1. Remember, the Festival of First fruits symbolized the resurrection of Jesus Christ; now the Festival of Harvest symbolizes the events of the day of Pentecost in Acts 2.

2. These two festivals were celebrated fifty days apart. v16

3. In God's sovereignty, centuries before Christ ever came, God appointed these festivals to paint the prophetic picture of salvation for men.

4. What strong evidence for the sovereignty and the truthfulness of Holy Scripture!

5. The Festival of Harvest or Pentecost symbolized the great harvest of souls, of people giving their lives to God on the great Day of Pentecost when the Holy Spirit was to come upon men.

C. In looking at the prophetic picture of salvation, this is what we have seen this far:

1. The Passover symbolized God's salvation, the deliverance and redemption from the world by God.

2. The Festival of Unleavened Bread symbolized the need and urgency of the

believer to be freed from the world, freed from the enslavement of sin and death.

3. The Festival of First fruits symbolized the great hope for the believer as he marched toward the Promised Land, the great hope of being raised from the dead by the power of the resurrection of Jesus Christ.

As the believer marches to the Promised Land, he is to be filled with God's Spirit and bear strong testimony, seeking a great harvest of souls.

V. The Feast of Trumpets (*v 23-25*)

- The first four feasts that are given in Leviticus 23 describe for us the past work that God has done.
- The Passover = Christ died for our sins.
- The Feast of Unleavened Bread = Cleansing our lives and beginning our journey with Him.
- The Feast of First fruits = the resurrection of Jesus Christ and the hope of our resurrection.

- The Feast of Pentecost = the empowerment of the Holy Spirit for us to be a part of the great harvest of souls.
- These four feasts picture events of the past.
- We are living between the Feast of Pentecost and the Feast of Trumpets.
- There is a three-month gap between the two feasts.
- What were the Jewish people doing during this three-month interval?
- They were working the harvest field.
- This is what you and I need to be doing today.

A. Historical Observation

1. The Israelites had two silver trumpets that were used to call the people together and to signal directions as they journeyed to the Promised Land.

2. Trumpeters were apparently stationed at regular intervals to pass the signal through the entire camp.

3. Remember, there were two to four million Israelites camped around the Tabernacle.

Num 10:1-2 *"And the LORD spake unto Moses, saying, Make thee two trumpets of silver; of a whole piece shalt thou make them: that thou mayest use them for the calling of the assembly, and for the journeying of the camps."*

4. The Feast of Trumpets took place on the first day of the seventh month.

5. This is also called Rosh Hashanah: the beginning of the Jewish New Year.

6. All the information we are given here is that they were to gather together for a memorial.

B. Prophetic Application

1. For the nation of Israel.

a. God established the use of trumpets to communicate with the entire nation.

b. It would seem that this memorial would be to remind the nation that God would call them together and would fulfill all of His covenants with His chosen people.

c. This is prophesied in the Scriptures.

Joel 2:1 *"Blow ye the trumpet in Zion, and sound an alarm in my holy mountain: let all the inhabitants of the land tremble: for the day of the LORD cometh, for it is nigh at hand;"*

Joel 2:15 *"Blow the trumpet in Zion, sanctify a fast, call a solemn assembly:"*

Mat 24:29 *"Immediately after the tribulation of those days shall the sun be darkened, and the moon shall not give her light, and the stars shall fall from heaven, and the powers of the heavens shall be shaken:"*

Mat 24:31 *"And he shall send his angels with a great sound of a trumpet, and they shall gather together his elect from the four winds, from one end of heaven to the other."*

d. The nation of Israel is a scattered people and this memorial speaks of a time when God will gather His people together.

2. For the believers today.

a. The application for us today is that one day there will be a sound of a trumpet that will gather all believers unto the Lord.

b. We refer to this event as the Rapture.

c. Paul describes it for us in the N.T.

1 Th 4:16 *"For the Lord himself shall descend from heaven with a shout, with the voice of the archangel, and with the trump of God: and the dead in Christ shall rise first:"*

1 Cor 15:52 *"In a moment, in the twinkling of an eye, at the last trump: for the trumpet shall sound, and the dead shall be raised incorruptible, and we shall be changed."*

- We are waiting for the sound of the trumpet to call us out of this world.
- As we work and wait, we are to be involved in the harvest.
- Jesus is coming soon!
- Let's be faithful to serve Him now until He comes.
- Read: Leviticus 23:26-32

VI. Day of Atonement: *"Yom Kippur"*

- On the tenth day of the seventh month, everything in the camp of Israel ceased.
- Only one man was busy, and that man was the high priest.

- In Leviticus 16, we have a more detailed account of this observance. Note seven appointments.

  A. An Appointed Purpose

  1. What was the reason behind all that took place on the Day of Atonement?

  Lev 16:30 *"For on that day shall the priest make atonement for you, to cleanse you, that ye may be clean from all your sins before the LORD."*

  2. The word "*atonement*" is used 15 times in Leviticus 16.

  3. Among other things the Hebrew word means "*to cover*."

  4. Under the Old Testament economy, the blood of the sacrifices could not put away sin; it could only cover sin.

  5. The blood of bulls and goats could not take away sin; it could only cover sin. Only Jesus Christ's blood can take away sin.

  John 1:29 *"The next day John seeth Jesus coming unto him, and saith, Behold the Lamb of God, which taketh away the sin of the world."*

  6. Atonement was needed to deal with the

problem of sin.

7. God is holy and man is sinful.

8. Everything in the camp of Israel had been defiled by sin.

Lev 16:33 *"And he shall make an atonement for the holy sanctuary, and he shall make an atonement for the tabernacle of the congregation, and for the altar, and he shall make an atonement for the priests, and for all the people of the congregation."*

9. Even the holy tabernacle of God and the priesthood had been defiled by sin.

10. Of course, the people were also defiled by their sins.

Lev 16:21 *"And Aaron shall lay both his hands upon the head of the live goat, and confess over him all the iniquities of the children of Israel, and all their transgressions in all their sins, putting them upon the head of the goat, and shall send him away by the hand of a fit man into the wilderness:"*

a. "*Iniquity*" means crookedness - we are twisted out of shape and do not measure up to God's standard.

b. "*Transgression*" means rebellion - to cross over the line and go too far.

c. The word "*sin*" means to miss the mark - to err from our appointed goal.

d. The appointed purpose was to deal with the problem of sin.

e. The heart of every problem is the problem in the heart, and the problem in the heart is sin.

B. An Appointed Time

1. The priest did not do this every day of the week; he did this once a year.

Lev 16:2 *"And the LORD said unto Moses, Speak unto Aaron thy brother, that he come not at all times into the holy place within the veil before the mercy seat, which is upon the ark; that he die not: for I will appear in the cloud upon the mercy seat."*

2. Once a year the high priest was allowed to go into the Holy of Holies.

3. Every year this ceremony had to be repeated because the sacrifices could not take away sin.

4. Only the Lamb of God can take away sin.

Heb 9:24-26 "*For Christ is not entered into the holy places made with hands, which are the figures of the true; but into heaven itself, now to appear in the presence of God for us: Nor yet that he should offer himself often, as the high priest entereth into the holy place every year with blood of others; For then must he often have suffered since the foundation of the world: but now once in the end of the world hath he appeared to put away sin by the sacrifice of himself.*"

C. An Appointed Place

1. God had appointed only one place of sacrifice.

2. The tabernacle (*and later on the temple*) was God's appointed place.

3. There is only one appointed place of sacrifice as far as salvation is concerned - the cross where Jesus died.

1 Pet 2:24 "*Who his own self bare our sins in his own body on the tree that we, being dead to sins, should live unto righteousness: by whose stripes ye were healed.*"

4. Our Lord did not bear our sins in the Jordan River when he was baptized, because baptism is not the way of salvation.

5. Our Lord did not bear our sins in the temple as He was teaching, because education, as good as it is, is not God's way of salvation.

6. Christ bore our sins at the appointed place - the cross.

D. An Appointed Person

1. Not everyone was permitted to offer this sacrifice, only the high priest.

Leveticus 16:17 *"And there shall be no man in the tabernacle of the congregation when he goeth in to make an atonement in the holy place, until he come out, and have made an atonement for himself, and for his household, and for all the congregation of Israel."*

2. In other words, the high priest had to fulfill this responsibility alone.

a. First, he put off his beautiful garments.

b. Then he washed his flesh in water (*v. 4*) and put on the plain linen garments of a lowly servant.

3. This is a picture, of course, of our Lord Jesus.

a. There came a time when He laid aside His beautiful garments of glory.

b. He took upon Himself form of a servant.

c. He set Himself apart to do the will of God.

d. He came to earth and was obedient unto death.

4. God's appointed person for today is the Lord Jesus Christ, our glorified High Priest in heaven.

a. The Old Testament high priest had to offer sacrifices first for himself before he could offer sacrifices for the people.

b. Jesus needed no sacrifices for Himself, for He was holy, harmless, undefiled, separate from sinners.

c. Instead, He offered Himself as the sinless sacrifice.

E. An Appointed Price

1. Eighty-six times in the Book of Leviticus

the blood is mentioned.

2. It was not living animals that paid the price; it was dead animals offered as sacrifices.

3. The blood had to be shed.

4. Some people reject this teaching about blood.

Lev 17:11 *"For the life of the flesh is in the blood: and I have given it to you upon the altar to make an atonement for your souls: for it is the blood that maketh an atonement for the soul."*

5. This is God's plan, and we must accept it.

6. We are not saved by imitating Christ's example or by admiring His teaching.

7. We are not saved by His character.

8. We are saved by His shed blood.

9. His precious blood was the price of atonement..

F. An Appointed Procedure

1. The first thing the priest had to do was to kill the bullock for a sin offering for himself (*Lev. 16:11*)

2. Then he took the incense into the Holy of Holies.

a. This burning cloud of incense speaks of the glory of God.

b. Salvation is for the glory of God, not just for the good of man.

3. Then the high priest returned to the altar for the blood; he took it into the Holy of Holies and sprinkled it on the mercy seat, which was the ark of the covenant.

a. The two tables of the Law were in the ark, and Israel had broken that Law.

b. But the blood covered the broken Law.

c. It was the blood that made atonement.

4. Then the high priest came back to the altar where two goats were waiting.

a. He would kill one goat and take the blood into the Holy of Holies.

b. That blood he sprinkled on the mercy seat.

c. He then applied some of that blood to the brazen altar (*Lev. 16:18*)

d. The priest put his hands on the head of

the living goat and confessed the sins of the people of Israel.

e. Then that goat was taken out and turned loose in the wilderness, never to be seen again, "*As far as the east is from the west, so far hath he removed our transgressions from us.*" (**Ps. 103:12**)

f. These two goats together were called a sin-offering. One died; the other (*called the scapegoat*) was turned loose.

g. Jesus Christ died, He arose again, He went back to heaven.

h. Christ's sacrifice does not just cover sin - He takes our sins away.

i. The release of the scapegoat pictured the truth that the sins of the people had been taken away.

5. The high priest would then wash and clothe himself again in his garments, a picture of the fact that when our Lord finished His sacrificial work, He returned to heaven and took His throne of glory.

G. An Appointed Response

1. Finally, there was an appointed response on the part of the people.

2. What was this response?

Lev 23:27-28 *"Also on the tenth day of this seventh month there shall be a day of atonement: it shall be an holy convocation unto you; and ye shall afflict your souls, and offer an offering made by fire unto the LORD. And ye shall do no work in that same day: for it is a day of atonement, to make an atonement for you before the LORD your God."*

3. Salvation is not by our works.

a. The people did nothing.

b. The priest did it all.

c. They were not allowed to work.

d. Instead, they were to show sorrow for their sin and, by faith, to accept what God had provided for them.

e. The annual Day of Atonement speaks to us of God's love and God's grace.

f. There is nothing we can do. "*Not by works of righteousness which we have done, but according to his mercy he saved us*" (*Titus 3:5*).

H. The Prophetic Symbols of the Day of Atonement.

1. Spoke of the future atonement of Jesus Christ on Calvary.

2. Speaks of the future cleansing of Israel

a. We learned in our study of the Feast of Trumpets that one day God will call His elect people Israel back to the land of Palestine.

b. At the second coming of Christ, there will be a cleansing for the nation.

c. When the Lord Jesus Christ shall return, Israel shall look upon Him whom they have pierced, and they shall mourn because of their sin. Cf Zech. 12:10

d. As a result of this, there shall be a time of cleansing and purification, and the fountain shall be opened for sin and for uncleanness.

Zec 13:1 *"In that day there shall be a fountain opened to the house of David and to the inhabitants of Jerusalem for sin and for uncleanness."*

e. Paul reminds us of this in Romans.

Rom 11:25-27 *"For I would not, brethren, that ye should be ignorant of this mystery, lest ye should be wise in your own conceits; that blindness in part is happened to Israel, until the fulness of the Gentiles be come in. And so all Israel shall be saved: as it is written, There shall come out of Sion the Deliverer, and shall turn away ungodliness from Jacob: For this is my covenant unto them, when I shall take away their sins."*

3. The Future Cleansing of all Believers

"Husbands, love your wives, even as Christ also loved the church, and gave himself for it; that he might sanctify and cleanse it with the washing of water by the word, that he might present it to himself a glorious church, not having spot, or wrinkle, or any such thing; but that it should be holy and without blemish." (Eph. 5:25-27)

a. We must be honest and admit that we are far from glorious and far from being free of spots, wrinkles and blemishes.

b. But one of these days, we will be a glorious Church without spot and wrinkle and without blemish when we stand before the Lord.

c. This will take place after the Judgment Seat of Christ.

VII. The Feast of Tabernacles. v33-44

A. Historic Observation

1. The people were to celebrate the Festival of Tabernacles on the fifteenth day of the seventh month (*v.34*).

2. It was to last for seven days, a full week of festivities and worship.

3. The people were to begin with a sacred assembly on the first day, doing no work whatsoever (*v.35*).

4. They were to approach God for atonement (r*econciliation*) during each of the seven days, approach God through the Burnt Offering (*v.36*).

5. On the eighth day, they were to hold another sacred assembly to close the festival.

6. The body of the whole nation was called together to approach God for atonement or

reconciliation through another Burnt Offering (*v.36*).

7. Note that the importance of the Feast of Tabernacles and the other feasts was stressed:

a. They were all annual sacred assemblies for worship, a time when the whole nation was to assemble together to approach God (*v.37*).

b. They were for the purpose of approaching God for atonement or reconciliation through the sacrifices and offerings (*v.37*).

c. They were to be additional celebrations, not to replace a person's regular approach to God. They were to be in addition to all other approaches to God.

d. They were not to replace the freewill offerings, nor the regular Sabbath day worship, nor any other gift or offerings that the people brought to God.

e. They were, as stated, to be an additional period of worship or celebration of the LORD (*v.38*).

8. Note that the importance of the Feast of Tabernacles is reemphasized (*v.39,40*).

a. It was to be celebrated on the fifteenth day of the seventh month and last for seven days.

b. It was to be celebrated after the crops had been harvested.

c. Both the first day and the eighth day were to be days of rest.

9. Note that the people were to build booths or shelters from tree leaves on the first day.

a. They were to live in these booths or shelters for seven days (*v.40, 42*).

b. The festival was to be a celebration of great joy and rejoicing before the Lord (*v.40- 41*).

c. The festival was to be a lasting, permanent law (*v.41*).

B. Historical Purpose for the Festival:

1. It was to teach all descendants that their ancestors had to live in booths when God delivered them out of Egypt.

2. Note that this was a symbol of how

temporary this world is.

3. Also note the warning of God: *"I am the Lord your God"* (*v.43*).

4. God expected His people to celebrate the Festival of Tabernacles.

5. If they failed, His judgment would fall upon them.

6. He is the Lord their God, able to execute judgment.

C. Application for us Today

1. God Wants His People to Have Joy

a. God wanted to remind the people that He had led them out of Egypt, had led them through the wilderness, and had been good to them.

b. The Feast of Tabernacles was a reminder to the Jewish people that everything they had came from God.

c. We need to remember this also.

1) Sometimes folks in church take everything for granted - the church building, the ministry.

2) But we need to remember that people

sacrificed, worked and gave that the building and ministry might be here.

3) Look back and be grateful for God's past mercies.

d. God also wants us to be grateful for the present blessings.

1) The Feast of Tabernacles was a harvest festival.

2) So Israel could look back and be thankful for God's provision, protection and direction.

3) They once lived in booths - now they were living in houses.

4) They once had to wander -now they were settled down.

5) They once had to ask Him for water - now they had plenty of water.

6) They could rejoice over past and present mercies from the generous hand of God.

7) We need to be reminded to enjoy what God has given us, and use it for His glory and for the good of others.

2. Joy Always Follows Cleansing

a. The Day of Atonement was followed by the Feast of Tabernacles.

b. Nothing robs us of joy like sin.

Psa 51:12 *"Restore unto me the joy of thy salvation; and uphold me with thy free spirit."*

c. Sin robs us of joy, but joy always follows cleansing.

d. This was true of the Prodigal Son; when he went home, and the father received him and forgave him, and there was great joy.

e. First the cleansing and then the joy.

f. The same is true for us today, first sin has to be taken care of, and then there can be joy and happiness.

g. God wants His people to have joy, and joy follows cleansing.

3. Joy Leads to Sacrifice

a. During the Feast of Tabernacles, nearly 200 different animals were sacrificed.

b. Numbers 29 gives you the details on this.

c. When we are joyfully thankful to God, sacrifice is no problem.

d. When we are happy in the Lord, rejoicing in His goodness, it is no problem at all to share what God gives us.

e. Jesus Christ became poor that we might be rich (*cf. 2 Cor. 8:9*).

4. The Greatest Joy Is Yet to Come

a. The Feast of Tabernacles is a picture of the future kingdom when Jesus shall reign.

Zec 14:4 *"And his feet shall stand in that day upon the mount of Olives, which is before Jerusalem on the east, and the mount of Olives shall cleave in the midst thereof toward the east and toward the west, and there shall be a very great valley; and half of the mountain shall remove toward the north, and half of it toward the south."*

Zec 14:9 *"And the LORD shall be king over all the earth: in that day shall there be one LORD, and his name one."*

Zec 14:16 *"And it shall come to pass, that every one that is left of all the nations which came against Jerusalem shall even go up from year to year to worship the King, the LORD of hosts, and to keep the feast of tabernacles."*

b. The Feast of Tabernacles will be a time of great rejoicing.

c. The greatest joy is yet to come, when you and I will enter into the glory of the Lord, when His Kingdom is established.

d. Let's not fix our hearts on the joys of this world because they will not last.

e. And let's not get discouraged because we are going through some difficulty; it will not last either.

Psa 30:5b *"...Weeping may endure for a night, but joy cometh in the morning."*

f. Jesus is coming soon; He will establish His Kingdom, and we shall reign with Him.

Rev 20:6 "Blessed and holy is he that hath part in the first resurrection: on such the second death hath no power, but they shall be priests of God and of Christ, and shall reign with him a thousand years."

CHAPTER NINETEEN

OVERCOMERS

It is the overcomers who will inherit the kingdom of God.Who is an overcomer? An overcomer is the one who has accepted and believed that Jesus Christ is the Son of the Living God.

1 John 5:4-5 *"For whatever is born of God overcomes the world; and this is the victory that has overcome the world—our faith. Who is the one who overcomes the world, but he who believes that Jesus is the Son of God?"*

An overcomer is someone who has been born of God, born again. How do we become born again? This is same question Nicodemus asked the Master and He answered in John 3:3 *"Jesus answered and said unto him, Verily, verily, I say unto thee, Except a man be born again, he cannot see the kingdom of God."*

John 1:12 (*WEB) "But as many as received him, to them he gave the right to become God's children, to those who believe in his name:"*

We need to receive Jesus Christ and confess Him

as our Lord and Personal Savior and then we become children of God and are saved.

Romans 10:9 (*NLT*) *"If you confess with your mouth that Jesus is Lord and believe in your heart that God raised him from the dead, you will be saved."*

Galatians 3:26 (*NASB*) *"For you are all sons of God through faith in Christ Jesus."*

Galatians 4:5-7 (*ESV*) *"To redeem those who were under the law, so that we might receive adoption as sons. [6] And because you are sons, God has sent the Spirit of his Son into our hearts, crying, "Abba! Father!" [7] So you are no longer a slave, but a son, and if a son, then an heir through God."*

The revelation of your identity is the access to your inheritance. You need to see where you are going before you can enter. You need to know your destination.

John 3:5 (*NLT*) *"Jesus replied, "I assure you, no one can enter the Kingdom of God without being born of water and the Spirit."*

Ephesians 5:25-26 (*NIV*) *"Husbands, love your wives, just as Christ loved the church and gave himself up for her to make her holy, cleansing her by the washing with water through the word,"*

John 15:3 (*NIV*) *"You are already clean because of the word I have spoken to you."*

1 John 5:6 (*ESV*) *"This is he who came by water and blood—Jesus Christ; not by the water only but by the water and the blood. And the Spirit is the one who testifies, because the Spirit is the truth."*

John 17:17 (*NIV*) *"Sanctify them by the truth; your word is truth."*

John 16:33 these things I have spoken to you that in me you may have peace, in the world, you will have tribulation but be of cheer, I have overcome the world. Amen

John 4:4 (*BLB*) *"You are of God, little children, and have overcome them, because the One in you is greater than the one in the world."*

We need to receive Jesus Christ who is the Overcomer to overcome. *"And they overcame him by the blood of the Lamb, and by the word of their testimony; and they loved not their lives unto the death."* (*Revelation 12:11*)

1 John 5:8 (*AKJV*) *"And there are three that bear witness in earth, the Spirit, and the water, and the blood: and these three agree in one."*

Romans 8:14 *"For as many as are led by the Spirit of*

God, they are the sons of God."

Let us take a look at what made our Master Jesus Christ an Overcomer.

Luke 1:35 *"And the angel answered and said unto her, The Holy Ghost shall come upon thee, and the power of the Highest shall overshadow thee: therefore also that holy thing which shall be born of thee shall be called the Son of God."*

Titus 3:4-6 (*NIV*) *"But when the kindness and love of God our Savior appeared, he saved us, not because of righteous things we had done, but because of his mercy. He saved us through the washing of rebirth and renewal by the Holy Spirit, whom he poured out on us generously through Jesus Christ our Savior,"*

John 3:6 *"That which is born of the flesh is flesh; and that which is born of the Spirit is spirit."*

John 4:23 (*ESV*) *"But the hour is coming, and is now here, when the true worshipers will worship the Father in spirit and truth, for the Father is seeking such people to worship him."*

Jesus Christ arrived on earth as the Son of God. Your identity as the Son of God makes you a heir of God and grants you access to the authority and kingdom.

In the testing of Jesus Christ, it was directed to the Son of God. The enemy is mad at our identity as the sons of God. So Jesus is conscious of His identity as the Son of God.

Our Identity as the temple of God makes us an overcomer. We must be aware that we carry God's presence.

John 14:23 *"Jesus answered and said to Him, if anyone loves me, He will keep my word and my Father will love Him and we will come to Him and make our Home with him."*

John 17:21(*ESV*) *"That they may all be one, just as you, Father, are in me, and I in you, that they also may be in us, so that the world may believe that you have sent me."*

John 17:23 *"I in them, and thou in me, that they may be made perfect in one; and that the world may know that thou hast sent me, and hast loved them, as thou hast loved me."*

God in you, Emmanuel with us, Jesus Christ received and believed has made you the temple of God.

I Corinthian 6:19 (*ESV*) *"Or do you not know that your body is a temple of the Holy Spirit within you, whom you have from God? You are not your own,"*

You are the Body of Christ. Think about it for a minute. If we are the body of Christ, then it means our hands are hands of Christ, our feet is the feet of Christ, our tongue and our whole being is the Body of Christ. This revelation of being the Body of Christ gives us courage and confidence in prayer.

You are the Bride of Christ. You are Mrs. Jesus Christ. The apple of God's eye. He loves you with an everlasting love.

You are a king and a priest.*1 Peter 2:9, Revelations 1:6* and has made us kings and priest to His God and Father, to Him be glory and dominion forever and ever Amen. What are we expected to do as kings and priest? As priest we are expected to offer sacrifices of praise and worship our Father in Heaven in the beauty of His Holiness. Jesus Christ lived a life of worship and praise to the Father. Praise and worship are the sacrifices which brings God down into our everyday lives. Praise and worship will make us overcomers. Joshua overcame Jericho by praise. Jehoshaphat won the battle by praise.

As a king, we are expected to talk with authority. Jesus Christ knew He is a King and talked with authority in prayers. He addressed the dead and they arose, spoke to the seas and the storm and they became calm.

Luke 4:36 (*AKJV) "And they were all amazed, and spoke among themselves, saying, What a word is this! for with authority and power he commands the unclean spirits, and they come out."*

Revelation 2:7 (*ESV*) *"He who has an ear, let him hear what the Spirit says to the churches. To the one who conquers I will grant to eat of the tree of life, which is in the paradise of God.'"*

Revelation 2:11(*ESV*) *"He who has an ear, let him hear what the Spirit says to the churches. The one who conquers will not be hurt by the second death.'"*

Revelation 2:17 (*WEB*) *"...To him who overcomes, to him I will give of the hidden manna, and I will give him a white stone, and on the stone a new name written, which no one knows but he who receives it."*

Revelation 2:26 (*ESV*) *"The one who conquers and who keeps my works until the end, to him I will give authority over the nations,"*

Revelations 3:5 (*DBT*) *"He that overcomes, he shall*

be clothed in white garments, and I will not blot his name out of the book of life, and will confess his name before my Father and before his angels."

Revelation 3:12 (*NASB*) *"He who overcomes, I will make him a pillar in the temple of My God, and he will not go out from it anymore; and I will write on him the name of My God, and the name of the city of My God, the new Jerusalem, which comes down out of heaven from My God, and My new name."*

Revelations 21:2-7 (*NASB*) *"And I saw the holy city, new Jerusalem, coming down out of heaven from God, made ready as a bride adorned for her husband. And I heard a loud voice from the throne, saying, "Behold, the tabernacle of God is among men, and He will dwell among them, and they shall be His people, and God Himself will be among them*[*, and He will wipe away every tear from their eyes; and there will no longer be any death; there will no longer be any mourning, or crying, or pain; the first things have passed away."And He who sits on the throne said, "Behold, I am making all things new." And He *said, "Write, for these words are faithful and true." Then He said to me, "It is done. I am the Alpha and the Omega, the beginning and the end. I will give to the one who thirsts from the spring of the water of life* *without cost. He who overcomes will inherit these things, and I will be his God and he will be My son."*

I John 5:4 (*WEB*) *"For whatever is born of God overcomes the world. This is the victory that has overcome the world: your faith."*

In conclusion, we overcome when we receive Christ and confess our faith in Him. We overcome when we realize our identity in Him. We overcome by the Spirit of God who is our Helper. We overcome by the Blood of the Lamb that prevailed. Finally, the Presence of God makes us overcomers. This is our predestination.

ABOUT THE AUTHOR

EMe Chijioke Eze is a data analyst. He is a graduate of Information Technology, Aptech Institute, Nigeria. He works with RCI as an Escalation Specialist Resolving Issues. He is a product of Dr. David Oyedepo and Dr. Paul Enenche Ministries, and a lover of Jesus Christ, having experienced the glorious and miraculous of God's presence. He lives in Mexico City where he works as a missionary.

ABOUT THE BOOK

Predestination is a work born out of the author's total experience and continuous communion with God in the most holy place, beholding the glory of God.

This masterpiece will empower you to enter into your rest and experience the unprecedented manifestation of God's glory when you read it prayerfully.

It is not just my contribution to the body of Christ but meat for every matured believer. This work of the Spirit will fill you with all you ever need to discover your destiny in Christ and fulfill your divine destiny.

www.ingramcontent.com/pod-product-compliance
Lightning Source LLC
LaVergne TN
LVHW041318080426
835513LV00008B/511

* 9 7 8 9 7 8 5 0 4 9 6 5 7 *